Flight from the Croft

Flight from the Croft

Bill Innes

Whittles Publishing

Published by
Whittles Publishing Ltd.,
Dunbeath,
Caithness, KW6 6EG,
Scotland, UK

www.whittlespublishing.com

ISBN 978-184995-397-9

Printed and bound by CPI Group (UK) Ltd, Croydon, CR0 4YY

Contents

Prologue vii

Glasgow University Air Squadron 1

National Service 7

British European Airways 30

John Welford 65

The Heron and Air Ambulance 70

The Viscount 79

The Comet 95

The Tiger Club 107

Romance 118

Vanguard 121

Tridents 142

Boeing 757 160

Moving on: Air 2000 170

Canada 3000 176

Air 2000 184

Alitalia 197

Fear of Flying 204

Epilogue 210
Appendix 1: Early aviation in Scotland 229

Prologue

The sonorous song of a Merlin engine echoed from the steep flanks of Glencoe as the Spitfire flashed her shapely wings, banking to follow the contours of the glen. A seven-year-old boy gazed in wonder at the sheer beauty and grace of her and an improbable ambition was born.

The year was 1940. Fired by hero worship for the dashing pilots of the RAF and their deeds of derring-do, I dreamt of roaming the clouds in such a thrilling machine. However as life's events conspired, the dream seemed doomed. Later that year, my elderly father died suddenly. My mother was left to bring up two young boys in a lonely little cottage half a mile from the nearest village on a widow's pension of ten shillings (50p) a week. Even in those days that was a pitiful

Spitfire MK 14. © Vickers Armstrong

The Bowie house in the early '50s.

amount and the strain on my mother brought on a nervous breakdown. Eventually my five-year-old brother and I were fostered out to a family even further removed from civilisation in the island of South Uist in the Outer Hebrides.

In those days the island way of life was a good fifty years behind the rest of the country. The new home we two waifs had been so kindly offered by the Bowie family was a little three-roomed thatched cottage with three-foot-thick stone walls and tiny, deep-set windows. There was no electricity or running water – nor any bathing or toilet facilities. Lighting was by paraffin lamp and all water had to be carried in buckets from a well 200 metres away. Yet old Mrs Bowie, whom we called 'Granny', had brought up eleven children in that house. By all accounts, she treated us with the same kindness she had shown her own family. Her children were now adults and scattered all over by the demands of war service – the only exception being her 19-year-old son Peter who had been excused military call-up to carry on the essential work of the croft.

That work involved arduous manual labour in a never-ending battle against the Hebridean weather. Horses were still used to draw a cart and single-furrow plough. Hay and corn were cut by scythe and sheaves were bound and stacked by hand. For all that, Peter loved his work and the islanders, united in poverty and rich in community spirit, seemed not to realise they were materially poor. In today's prosperity, some islanders appear reluctant to admit that times were once so hard, although they have every right to be proud of the improvement in their standard of living. Fortunately, some of that community spirit still survives in this era of homes with every mod con.

It has to be admitted that a natural streak of idleness made me a reluctant crofter. Dawn to dusk manual labour was never going to be to the taste of one who, given any opportunity, much preferred to bury his head in a book. That did eventually pay off as I gradually inched up the academic ladder. The only secondary school in South Uist in those days was a corrugated iron three-roomed building in Daliburgh. It was only nine miles away but the lack of buses or personal transport made it necessary to board close to the school for the whole term. However basic the school building, Scottish state education was then rated amongst the finest in the world. At the age of eleven we were already studying Shakespeare and Latin.

Progress beyond third year meant moving to the senior secondary school in mainland Fort William. There was no possibility of anyone leaving the croft to accompany me so at fourteen I climbed aboard the overnight ferry, suitcase in hand, on my own. The journey home might take over thirty hours so boarding for the term was inevitable. The consequent bouts of extreme homesickness made for some miserable early months but I eventually accumulated the necessary Higher passes to qualify for university. In those days, very few from the island ever went to university and it is to the Bowie family's eternal credit that they encouraged my ambition. For them it was a poor bargain. Not only did it entail extra expense, which they could ill afford, but they also lost a pair of hands around the croft just as I came to an age when I might have made a real contribution. It was to prove the most generous gift of my lifetime. Granny was asked by a concerned neighbour:

'What good will it do for you that he is getting all that education?'

Her simple reply:

'It might do some good for somebody!'

My university ambitions aimed no higher than the ordinary degree which would qualify me to become a primary teacher back in the islands. In those days it was deemed perfectly normal for men to teach primary school children. The dream of becoming headmaster of the little two-roomed local school at Howmore seemed the pinnacle of possible achievement. That other totally impossible dream – of becoming a pilot – had moved even further beyond the reach of a barefoot ragamuffin in the time capsule of Uist.

It was during my time at university that the fairy godmother waved her wand. As part of an air-mindedness programme for graduates, the Royal Air Force has reserve air squadrons at major universities. Not only are students taught for free but they are given expenses as well. Having applied more in hope than expectation, I was surprised to find myself going through aptitude tests and selection procedures with a group from some of Glasgow's finest private schools. Compared to them I was naïve and unsophisticated, but the RAF has always valued keenness. The enthusiasm shining in my eyes must have swung the day.

Glasgow University Air Squadron

This was how Cadet Pilot Innes found himself travelling to Scone to be introduced to that classic little trainer plane, the deHavilland Chipmunk. Although Scone was still a grass airfield in those days it had a major training role in the Royal Air Force Volunteer Reserve, in which the Air Squadron played a part.

Our accommodation was in wartime dormitory huts which, scorning any concession to insulation, were singularly ill-suited to the rigours of the Scottish winter. The central heating system consisted of a small cylindrical stove. Centrally located, admittedly, but otherwise totally unequal to the task of raising the temperature of a basic building. which might have been expressly designed as a primitive device for radiating heat to the freezing night sky. Even in bed it seemed impossible to warm the icy cold sheets to anything approaching comfort level. My fellow would-be pilots

Early days in the Chipmunk

were a fascinating bunch drawn from a variety of disciplines. Nigel knew all the words to *Largo al Factotum* from Rossini's *Barber of Seville* and would go on to be a future professor of history; Ken a much respected family GP. Peter displayed a scientific bent that found practical expression in an improvised bed-warmer. Consisting as it did of a naked light bulb inside an old bean tin, it would have had some difficulty meeting modern 'Elf 'n Safety' requirements. With no such makeshift comfort myself, I got little sleep that first night and tossed restlessly in delicious yet terrifying anticipation of what tomorrow might bring.

Morning eventually arrived and I struggled into my new stiff blue battledress and assembled my new kit of flying overalls and leather helmet complete with oxygen mask and goggles. Not that I was likely to need oxygen in the Chipmunk but the mask also incorporated the microphone for radio and intercom. After breakfast we walked down the flight line to the hut that served as the air squadron offices. The elegant little Chipmunks were already buzzing about the field and I watched enviously as one glided across the hedge. As its wheels kissed the grass in a perfect three-point touchdown it seemed impossible that I could ever achieve such a level of expertise. There were many other planes as well, from high wing army Austers to Airspeed Oxfords and Avro Ansons. The latter two not only looked enormous but had twin engines to cope with. Clearly their pilots had to be supermen indeed. Tucked away in one corner of the hangar was a strange and interesting beast – the one-off Kay gyroplane with its helicopter-like rotor. I believe it still resides in the National Museum of Scotland in Edinburgh.

The actual business of setting off in an aeroplane was an immensely complicated ritual. With my instructor I embarked on a minute external inspection of our machine – silver-coloured with bright yellow stripes on fuselage and wings to mark its training role. Tyres were kicked and ailerons wiggled. The engine had to be primed with petrol and cowlings carefully re-fastened. Eventually I struggled into the many straps of the parachute, which dangled beneath my bottom until I clambered clumsily into the front cockpit where it conveniently acted as a seat cushion. I then connected myself to the radios via the massive plug dangling from my leather helmet and did up a further set of seat straps. By the time I had latched my oxygen mask tightly to the helmet and donned the RAF's two sets of gloves, I felt like the proverbial trussed chicken – oven-ready in my gently perspiring state.. There were more checks of instruments and switches and radios to be painstakingly worked through until the magic moment we were cleared to start. With a loud bang from the Chipmunk's cartridge starter the Gypsy Major burst into vibrant life – as did some of the instruments which had hitherto been as inert as the handbook pictures I had pored over for hours.

I cannot pretend that my first year was an easy one. Lack of continuity, constant instructor changes and a basic lack of confidence meant it took me nearly fifteen hours to go solo. Although I was allowed to fly an aeroplane solo before I could drive a car, at the end of the year I was given the humiliating assessment of 'below average'. There is little doubt that, had I joined the Air Force proper, my fledgling flying career would have been terminated before it had properly begun.

My salvation was that the air squadrons were less demanding. A struggler could be tolerated – even if only to be the butt of squadron jokes. Confidence is vital to a pilot and mine undoubtedly suffered badly. With the benefit of 20/20 hindsight, it is useful to look back and realise why it took me such a long time to find my feet.

Delightful aircraft though the Chipmunk is, it has one defect as a trainer. Student and instructor sit in tandem, with the latter in the rear cockpit which means that he or she cannot monitor the student's visual scan. Budding pilots should learn to fly by reference to the visual horizon and other outside cues. However, in my enthusiasm I had swotted up religiously on the flying instruments and tried to fly by them right from the start. An inexperienced instrument pilot makes all sorts of minor fiddly adjustments which can be uncomfortable for a more competent passenger.

It was only when I started the instrument flying section of the course that my misdirected efforts eventually paid off. Training was conducted with the student under a hood so that the aircraft instruments were the only source of information. As this was little different to my standard operation, I sailed through the test for the RAF's White Card basic all-weather qualification – much to my instructor's surprise. The other area in which I attracted more praise than criticism was in aerobatics which of course *had* to be flown by reference to the horizon.

Eventually I achieved the prized 'above average' assessment. Later it became standard for primary trainers such as the Provost and Bulldog to have side-by-side seating so that the instructor could monitor the student more directly.

The air squadron played a further important part in my general education. The offices in Bute Gardens housed one of the best and most exclusive student clubs at the university. While the subsidised prices in the cocktail bar greatly accelerated the normally steep student learning curve on alcohol tolerance, the formal dining-in nights were an eye-opening introduction to the social graces required of a potential RAF officer. Elaborately dressed tables and rituals of toasts and passing of the port were a far cry from the humble meals at home – where fingers were still used more often than forks. The traditional drink-fuelled mess games afterwards always seemed rather childish, although this was possibly just because I was not very good at them. They had, however, been vital relaxation therapy for the young men who

3

had diced with death daily in the still-so-recent war. Some of the survivors were now our instructors. The real icing on the cake came every summer when the squadron decamped to a regular RAF station, preferably as far from Glasgow as possible. I still have in my possession a warrant for a journey from Lochboisdale in South Uist to St. Eval in Cornwall, which must be one of the longest journeys possible within the UK. These camps gave us the opportunity of a fortnight's continuous training while experiencing the civilised lifestyle of the officers' mess.

However, the move to large RAF airfields introduced us to another complication of aviation which Scone (still a grass field in those days) had spared us: crosswinds. Prior to WWII, very few aerodromes had runways so take-offs and landings could be conducted in any direction, depending on the wind that day. Although the three runways of a standard 50s RAF airfield provided six different take-off and landing directions, the prevailing wind might not be directly aligned with any of them and approaches were made crabbing into the wind at an angle to the runway centre line. For fast-landing jets this was not much of a problem, particularly as a tricycle undercarriage aircraft would straighten itself out on touchdown even if landed while still crabbing.

Unfortunately for us, this was not the case for the much slower, tailwheel Chipmunk. The geometry of a tailwheel aircraft gives it an innate tendency to weathercock into wind. On a normal Chipmunk take-off, the effect of propeller wash over the tail gave a tendency to swing to the right so left rudder was required

Author at summer camp, RAF St Eval, Cornwall in 1954.

4

in correction. If the wind was also on the right, even more rudder was required. Furthermore, when the tail was raised, this right-bearing tendency was aggravated by the gyroscopic effect of changing the plane of orientation of the propeller. It was essential to ensure one had good rudder control before raising the tail. However, all that was relatively simple compared with the dreaded crosswind landing technique. The RAF taught a method whereby the pilot crabbed the aircraft down the runway centre line until the flare. At the very last moment rudder was to be applied so that the aircraft landed pointing down the runway – ideally on all three wheels.

All very well in theory but in practice the technique required a measure of fine judgement usually only acquired at the cost of some heart-stopping moments along the way. Even if successfully executed, there was no time to relax. Tail down, there is less airflow over the rudder and its control correspondingly reduced. Any subsequent swing might cause a departure from the runway or even that humiliating rotation known as a 'ground loop'. Taxiing in strong winds was also a problem. Rudder at slow speed had even less effect but a partial application of hand brake could provide differential braking through the pedals. The danger here was that braking and tail wheel aircraft make for an uneasy combination. As many a pilot has discovered to his cost, it is all too easy to apply too much brake and tip the machine up on its nose. The consequent expensive grinding noise of prop on tarmac has been the premature swansong of many a promising career. Small wonder that I returned from my first solo experience of a gusty wind on tarmac a quivering wreck, gratefully abandoning my no-smoking policy to calm my shattered nerves!

However, the compensations at these summer camps were many, including the thrill of scrounging rides in some of the RAF's aircraft of the time. RAF Waddington provided a glimpse of recent history when I was allowed a passenger flight in a Lincoln bomber on exercise. As successor to the Lancaster, it gave a small insight into the life of bomber crews but without the nerve-numbing terror of real war. RAF Wittering had Canberra twin-engined bombers which were to have a long and successful career within the RAF and the United States Air Force. At the time, they were still state-of-the-art and it was a thrill to be able to view the earth from over 40,000 feet for the first time. My pilot told me how he had been intercepted on a previous training exercise by Meteor fighters. His simple response had been to open the throttles and out-climb them. However, nemesis overtook him a few days later when he was caught by one of the latest Hawker Hunters which he was unable to shake off. My favourite memory is of a trip in a Canberra flown by the Wing Commander Flying at Wittering. As the senior operational pilot on the base, he took advantage of his position to do a spectacular low pass over the airfield. It was further confirmation of my early view that service flying promised to be exciting and fun.

That, however, was still but a dream. On the academic side, I had scraped together the necessary passes to graduate in the summer of 1954. The sensible course was to continue with my original plan and train to be a primary school teacher and so, that autumn, I began a one-year post-graduate course at Jordanhill Teacher Training College (now part of Strathclyde University). Although the course and practice teaching were both enjoyable, morale was not improved when one of the lecturers pointed out that we were unlikely to see any promotion for the first 18 years. Over that timescale our starting salary of £12 a week would rise to a heady £18. Mind you, to put that in perspective, footballers of the time earned about £14 a week!

National Service

National Service was seen by many as an arduous and time-wasting interruption in their lives. For many others, including this writer, it was a life-enhancing and life-changing experience.

Thanks to my time with the Air Squadron, I was accepted for pilot training in the RAF. While ex-University Air Squadron (UAS) entrants were given a quicker route towards the coveted wings, we still had to first undergo the obligatory purgatory of bull, barracks and drill under the hawk-eyed gaze of regular RAF NCOs (non-commissioned officers), who paid scant regard to any officer-cadet status. (We had been granted the rank of Acting Pilot Officer, having previously thought that Pilot Officer was the lowest form of commissioned life in the RAF). September 1955 found me at RAF Kirton-on-Lindsey being initiated into the importance of squared-off beds, shining barrack room floors and gleaming footwear.

All that was forgotten in our delight at learning we were to be the first ex-UAS course to be sent to Canada for training. Canada had adapted its important wartime training tradition to accept students from all the NATO countries. Our extremely basic RAF salary of £12 a month was to be almost trebled by additional allowances to cope with the difference in cost of living. Furthermore, our sartorial standards were massively improved by the addition of the RAF parade dress uniform to our rough National Service standard issue. Its smooth barathea cloth and peaked hat by Bates of Jermyn Street in London were deemed essential to our new role as RAF representatives abroad. Even more exciting was the tropical climes khaki drill uniform which held promise of warmer summer temperatures in Canada.

Empress of Scotland *at Liverpool.* © *Canadian Pacific*

Thus it was that a motley bunch of graduates from Bristol, London, Cambridge, Durham, Glasgow and Manchester found ourselves assembling in Liverpool in December 1955 to board the Canadian Pacific SS *Empress of Scotland* bound for Montreal. Our ship was a grand old lady of the pre-war era. In those days she had been the *Empress of Japan* on the Pacific run from Vancouver. Unsurprisingly, the entry of Japan into WWII had prompted her re-naming. Her presence was all the more imposing for having three funnels – although the rearmost was, sadly, a fake.

In the mid-50s, Britain was still in the grip of post-war austerity. Our crossing of the Atlantic introduced us to the sort of luxury lifestyle some of us had only ever seen in the movies; the Air Force had booked us officer cadets in first class. The huge first-class dining room was as grand as that of any five-star hotel. The menus were just as spectacular for those of us accustomed to food shortages and rationing. Even breakfast could be stretched to seven courses!

It is regrettable that the jet airliner all but eliminated scheduled ocean crossings by ship. There is no doubt that the great liners provided the most civilised mode of trans-Atlantic travel. The clocks went back an hour a day over nearly a week of cosseted living, so there was no problem with jet lag as we entered the Saint Lawrence Estuary. There was great anticipation as we spotted houses on the shore which, unlike those in Scotland at the time, were resplendent in bright colours.

The first shock was when we were allowed ashore to stretch our legs in Quebec. '*Touristes!*' hissed one shopkeeper to his wife on hearing our voices. Canada for us was still part of the British Empire; no one had bothered to enlighten me that the Quebecois spoke French!

Eventually we disembarked in Montreal and dragged our new steel RAF trunks onto a train for the next part of our journey – through the snow to London, Ontario. Another culture shock ensued for those accustomed in winter to huddling round coal fires and travelling in the freezing corridor trains of British Rail. Canadian trains were centrally heated to a degree which seemed tropical to us. I was nearly chucked off the train for trying to open a window which proved to be double-glazed – an unheard-of refinement back home.

RCAF London was a transit centre where new intakes were allocated to the four main initial training stations across Canada. It was difficult to sleep once more in

Harvard 4 re-fuelling.

barrack-type rooms but I can still recall the excitement of hearing the mournful, familiar-only-from-the movies sound of the steam train whistles. We were abroad!

Eventually, our course (numbered 5509, being the ninth course of the year) was allocated to RCAF Centralia which was about twenty-five miles north of London. Others departed to far-flung spots with exotic names like Portage-le-Prairie and Moose Jaw. At Centralia, we started ground school and then were introduced to one of the most famous trainer planes of all time – the North American AT6, better known in Britain and Canada as the Harvard. The flight line at Centralia had serried ranks of them, all gleaming yellow with Canada's maple leaf emblem replacing the centre disc of the RAF roundel.

Thousands of pilots round the world had graduated to the allied air forces of WWII via this classic beast – and indeed a beast it seemed to me after the Chipmunk. Being larger, heavier, more powerful and faster, it was an aircraft which demanded respect. In particular, the earlier models were notorious for being difficult to keep straight in crosswind landings. Like the Chipmunk, the Harvard was a tail wheel aircraft with the same inbuilt tendency to weathercock into wind. In any such deviation not immediately corrected, the Harvard was even more likely to embark on the ignominious rotation of a ground loop which could wipe off the undercarriage and call down the wrath of the establishment on the unfortunate student.

Fortunately for us, our section had the later Harvard 4 which had a lockable tail wheel. This invaluable modification limited the airport trolley castoring characteristics of the earlier models; undoubtedly saving some of us from potential embarrassment. Our course was now a polyglot mixture of cadets from the NATO

countries. We were joined by French, Belgian, Dutch and even Canadian students.

Accommodation improved to twin-bedded rooms, spartan of furnishing but centrally heated against the Canadian winter. Snow lay around at a depth that would have been sufficient to cause total chaos back in Britain but the Canadians were organised and equipped to deal with it. Massive blowers made sure that roads, tarmac and runways were kept clear. The food was a wonderful bonus after post-war austerity Britain – even if some of us never came to terms with pouring maple syrup over bacon. We had our own cadet mess to relax in but, status-wise, were still cadets who marched to the flight hangars and ground school. We continued to polish our square-bashing skills – and our uniform shoes.

I have to admit that I never came to love the Harvard. Despite my having acquired a modest expertise in aerobatics in the Chipmunk, our new trainer seemed a heavy brute by comparison. However, it was a much more sophisticated aeroplane with retractable undercarriage and propeller pitch controls to worry about. On take-off it emitted an utterly distinctive sonorous roar as the tips of the propeller went supersonic. Its comprehensive instrument panel was reminiscent of the WWII fighters for which it had served as the introduction for so many pilots. (Harvards have appeared in many war movies as stand-ins for more prestigious fighters). In particular, it was equipped with such toys as an Automatic Direction Finder (ADF) which had a needle that could be tuned to give a heading towards a radio beacon or a commercial radio station. The RAF of the time scorned such navigational fripperies, preferring to rely on VHF radio talk-downs. We, however, revelled in a device which, apart from proving invaluable in navigation, could also be tuned to local radio stations for the 'Top 50 in the Country and Western Hit Parade'. On solo flights, such a soundtrack transformed aerobatic practice into a mind-blowing experience!

While I did not distinguish myself in the aeroplane, my credit rating was redeemed by ground school. The RCAF used new-fangled multi-answer questions which suited my remember-by-association mind. Thus I found myself coming top in exams by virtue of being better at recognising the correct alternative.

In March 1956 we were given some leave for the Easter break. The most popular way of exploiting this was to hitchhike to nearby Detroit, the capital of the American car industry. The many drive-away agencies which delivered cars all over the States advertised for drivers who would deliver them for no reward other than the pleasure of having the use of a modern car for a few days. There was only one snag. Despite having taken some driving lessons in Glasgow, I did not have a full licence.

This was easily solved. In those days, Canadian driving licences were issued by the butcher in the nearby town of Exeter. He was happy to issue one on the strength of my British licence, oblivious to the fact that it was only provisional. It is true that he was supposed to check my skills with a circuit of the block, but even that modest requirement was waived when I disingenuously regretted that I had not brought my car that day. In a country where every red-blooded Canadian had a full licence in his or her teens, it never occurred to him that a 22-year-old pilot might be a motoring novice.

The author with 1954 Buick Riviera hardtop.

I had made friends with a likeable Canadian – Dick Murray – who was still only eighteen but already an experienced driver. However, you had to be over twenty one to be trusted with a drive-away car. We agreed to make a trip together. If I could sign for the car and get it out of the agency yard, he could take over around the corner and run the gauntlet of the Detroit traffic. At the heart of the thriving automobile industry, Detroit was still a vibrant city. So it was that I found myself behind the wheel of a massive-by-British-standards Buick Riviera hardtop, having never driven an automatic car before in my life. But the plan worked and off we set for North Carolina.

Having taken care of the tricky bits, Dick would hand over to me for the rolling expanses of the American freeways and turnpikes; roads the like of which we had not then begun to dream about in Britain. It was a wonderful introduction to the States in a car with a 5.3 litre engine which took it effortlessly to over 100 mph. On the roads, gas was cheap and motel rooms could be had for three or four dollars a night. We wove a wandering route through the northern states, made a detour to Kitty Hawk to pay homage to the Wright brothers and handed over the Buick in North Carolina with considerable regret. Further progress was by hitchhiking, which was still a common and safe practice. Patriotic Americans were particularly kind to anyone wearing uniform.

Our ultimate goal was Miami but the transit of the southern states was an eye-opener. It was our introduction to a form of apartheid just as rigid as that subsequently so criticised in South Africa. Whites had privileges and separate toilets; blacks were poor and had to ride in the backs of buses. After several car rides, we were eventually picked up by a truck driver from Arkansas with whom we covered the last 500 miles. The rig was impressive with its twenty gears and foghorn of a hooter in the roof, but we were taken aback by the contempt in his voice when he spoke of the 'coons'. Fortunately, my most enduring memory is of being welcomed to Florida by a spectacular sunset – the March air sweet with the heady scent of orange blossom.

We made our base in one of the art deco hotels of Miami Beach and took boat tours to marvel at the mansions and yachts of the rich. Naturally we felt a visit to Miami Airport was a must. In those happy pre-security days we wandered onto the tarmac and gazed wistfully at Constellations and DC7s – and lustfully at the unattainably glamorous hostesses walking out to them.

Our reverie was interrupted by a distinctive whining sound and into view taxied a Vickers Viscount 700. Nowadays it is difficult to appreciate what an enormous technological advancement the Viscount represented with its smoothly spinning turbines replacing the huge vibrating piston engines of its predecessors. This particular one belonged to British West Indian Airlines and my breast swelled with

Eastern Airlines Lockheed Constellation with cabin crew, Miami, March 1956.

BWIA Vickers Viscount 700 at Miami, 1956.

Miami International, March 1956.

patriotic pride. The Viscount is still the most successful British commercial aircraft of all time but its pedigree had made little impression on insular Americans who assumed any worthwhile technology had to be from the good old USA.

'So you guys have the Viss-count as well'?

The time came to explore the possibilities for the return journey The Florida holiday season of the 50s was almost exclusively a winter phenomenon as refugees from Canada and the northern states escaped the winter snows. Our stay in Miami Beach was affordable thanks to a dramatic post-Easter drop in prices coupled with an American tendency to offer good deals to service personnel. This was decades before the invasion by Brits and other Europeans who were prepared to brave the heat, humidity and thunderstorms of a Florida summer.

We discovered that Miami also had drive-away agencies, specialising in returning cars to those residents of the north who preferred to let the plane take the strain. We found ourselves entrusted with the 'top beast' from the General Motors stable – a Cadillac no less – to take all the way to Toronto. Luxurious certainly, but not as much fun as the Buick had been. It is not surprising that, more than sixty years later, the Riviera hardtop still has classic car status in the USA. Despite the Cadillac also being part of the General Motors stable, its handling, by comparison, was barge-like. As the weather returned to winter conditions on our journey north, I was badly caught out in snow. Through treading on the accelerator with too heavy a foot, I found myself broadside on to the potential traffic in the middle of a small town high street. My panicky attempt at skid correction via the power steering promptly reversed the process to present the other cheek, so to speak. We were only saved from disastrous consequences by the width of American streets and the lightness of traffic in the 50s.

As work resumed after the break, dramatic events started to unfold. An 18-year-old RAF cadet from another course had not returned from his leave. This would have been a major crime in any of the services, but it was most unusual in flight training where enthusiasm and keenness were the norm. When Cadet B**** eventually turned up several days later, it transpired that *en vacance* he had fallen for some siren whose charms were more seductive than those of the Harvard.

He was promptly incarcerated in the Guardroom to await the due wrath of the establishment. Presumably, however, the guards did not expect officer cadet criminals to require close supervision. At any rate, he was able to slip out of custody, walk down to the busy flight line and help himself to an idle Harvard without incurring any suspicion. He took off and then proceeded to terrorise the station with low passes for about an hour and a half.

Initially it was assumed that he must have suffered radio failure and an instructor took off to try and guide him down. But it rapidly became clear that our hero's trouble was entirely of his own making. All work ceased; the control tower and the school were evacuated. We stood aghast as the Harvard skimmed telephone lines and roof tops, occasionally vanishing behind buildings.

My friend Dick had departed earlier on a cross-country navigation exercise. As he was the last student legitimately airborne, initial suspicions cast him as the villain of the piece. When it was realised the lunatic was one of our own RAF colleagues, we assumed that the most likely – and most merciful – outcome of the adventure would be for him to dive the plane into the ground. However, the assault on the station eventually eased. The rogue Harvard landed and taxied sedately to its parking slot on the flight line. B**** climbed out, calmly slung his chute over his shoulder, and was cautiously surrounded by RCAF police before being hustled off to await the inevitable court martial.

The British cadets were just as outraged as the local higher brass. We felt that B**** had let us all down and caused considerable damage to the image of the RAF in the eyes of this international group. At one time or another we had all been guilty of some illicit low flying but usually in some remote spot that we hoped was far from the eyes of officialdom. This ego trip by an inexperienced pilot had not only been actively dangerous to a crowded station but we felt had been a grossly ill-mannered response to the generous hospitality of our hosts. We speculated on what punishment the court martial might impose and some regret was expressed that

Harvard low flying at Centralia, 1956.

boiling oil or burning at the stake were probably outwith its remit. The prosecuting lawyer was to be an RAF officer and his view of the severity of the offence was probably broadly in line with our own.

However, the Canadians were perhaps less inclined to deal harshly with a visitor to their shores. The defence counsel (RCAF) managed to tie the witnesses up in knots by exposing the well-known inability of lay people to estimate accurately the height of an aircraft. All that happened in the end was that B**** was sent back to the UK in disgrace – which was no doubt to have been his fate before his escapade anyway. Shortly after the court martial came to its conclusion in the absence of concrete evidence, one of the French cadets showed us his cine film of the event which clearly showed the Harvard disappearing behind buildings in its crazy dives. We fumed with impotent rage that it had not been available earlier.

Jets

The Harvard section of our aviation education ended with the usual passing out parade and a rising sense of excitement about the next stage: jet conversion. The standard RAF jet trainer of the time was the deHavilland Vampire which was essentially a very basic cockpit stuck on the front of a jet engine, fitted with a pair of wings connected by twin booms to the essential tail empennage. By comparison, the North American T33a was state of the art and was to become one of the all-time classics of the training world.

The original T33 was based on the American P80 single-seat fighter. The Canadian version, the T33a Silver Star, had its performance considerably enhanced through the fitting of a Rolls Royce Nene engine; so enhanced, in fact, that it out-performed the original fighter. RCAF T33a pilots had a lot of mischievous fun flying south across the US border, knowing they could easily outrun USAF P80 interceptors if they were provoked to climb to meet the 'threat'. One of Britain's earlier blunders had been to give the Nene engine to Russia where it so transformed the Mig15 fighter as to give the allies serious trouble during the Korean War.

As our course was destined for RCAF Gimli in Manitoba, one of their instructors arrived to give us a preliminary briefing. Appetite-whetting though his discourse was, there was a frisson of disquiet when he mentioned that they had had four fatal accidents that winter – a dismal record much worse than the other jet conversion units. Was it a jinx station, a jinx aircraft – or both? Time would tell.

Once more the steel trunks were packed and we embarked on a much longer train journey across the vastness of Canada. Even after spending five days and four

Canadian T33a poses over the Canadian half of Niagara Falls. © RCAF

nights on the Canadian Pacific Railway before arriving in Winnipeg, we were not yet within sight of the Rockies.

Gimli is chiefly remembered today for the extraordinary incident in the 1980s when an Air Canada Boeing 767, having run out of fuel, glided to a safe landing on one of its disused runways. In the 50s, it was a vibrant RCAF station alive with jet whine as T-birds practised landings on its very-much-used parallel runways.

In the RAF's eyes we were still unqualified Acting Pilot Officers but we were delighted to discover that, post-Harvard, the RCAF treated us as officers, with a very comfortable mess to relax in. The international mix on the course was enriched to include Turks and Danes. Impatient though we were to get our hands on the glamorous new toy, there was still the inevitable ground school where we were briefed on the aircraft systems and the use of such exotica as oxygen (essential) and ejection seats (hopefully unnecessary). There were new checklists and drills to memorise. On jet aircraft these can be lengthy, so we were particularly taken with the brevity of the plenum chamber fire checklist. The plenum chamber was above the fuel tank. Military jet fuel of the time was more explosive than that used by civilian jets today, so if the appropriate red light lit up, the drill was:

a) Max rate turn, looking back for smoke.

b) If smoke detected – eject!

The only drawback was that the American ejector seat fitted was old-fashioned compared to the Martin Baker seats in the contemporary RAF Vampire T11. Ejections below 1200 feet above ground were deemed unlikely to be successful. This was still a considerable improvement on the Vampire 5 and Meteor 7 trainers which had no ejector seats at all!

In all other respects the T33a, with its sophisticated electrical and hydraulic systems, was simply in a different league. The ailerons were hydraulic and the canopy and seat adjustment were electrical. The contrast was even more dramatic in cockpit layout. In British aircraft of the time the science of ergonomics seemed to be unknown. Switches and minor controls were scattered somewhat randomly around the basic instrument flying panel. The key instrument on this panel is the artificial horizon which displays the attitude and bank position of the aircraft in relation to the horizon. On British aircraft of the 50s period the gyro in this vital guide would topple in aerobatic manoeuvres, thereby rendering the instrument useless. Much time had to be devoted to training pilots in flying 'limited panel' without it, relying only on the basic airspeed, turn and slip, and vertical speed indicators. On the T33a, the fully-rotatable artificial horizon was unaffected by turning the aeroplane upside down. It was now a practical proposition to fly aerobatics in cloud or in the dark.

While every square inch of the tight-fitting T-Bird cockpit was filled with gauges and switches, there was evidence of considerable design input to the controls. The radio transmission switch was on top of the throttle under one's thumb. At full power on take-off, the flap selector fell conveniently under the index finger of the throttle hand. The control for the airbrakes was also part of the throttle lever. They were selected out with the little finger and stowed with a flick of the heel of the hand.

The entire trimming system for the controls was one button mounted under the pilot's thumb on the control column – wiggled fore and aft for elevator and sideways for aileron trim. (It was to be years before similar ideas became common on commercial aircraft.) Rudder pedals on single-engined jets were for resting your feet on.

The only flaw in this ergonomic bliss was that the undercarriage selector was hidden to the left of the pilot's seat. While that made it convenient to reach, it was fatally easy to select down without ensuring that the lever was locked. The result of any carelessness could be an embarrassing collapse on touchdown. After a few such incidents, a 'shake' test of the lever had to be included in the landing checklist.

Eventually the great day came for my first familiarisation flight. It was a standing joke on jet conversion that the early flights of ham-fisted ex-Harvard pilots were easily identified by the rocking of wings as they over-controlled the T-bird's hydraulic ailerons. But as we zoomed effortlessly past the Harvard's limit of 10,000 feet, I knew I was falling in love.

Compared to its lumbering predecessor, this aeroplane was a joy to handle. Even the early circuit-bashing for landing practice was fun because of the American 'closed pattern' technique used in the RCAF. Circuit training hitherto had been a boring rigmarole of flying a rectangular course to arrive on the final approach at about 800 feet for a staid and stabilised approach to the landing flare. (This was time-intensive when the object of the exercise is to practise as many landings as possible.) The T33 solution was much more exciting. On take-off, the wheels and flaps were retracted and the nose held down till the speed reached 210 knots (240 mph) – usually by the runway end. The pilot then pulled up vertically in a wingover onto the downwind leg. There were a few moments to complete the landing checks before you were abeam the runway threshold commencing a descending turn to roll the wings level very shortly before the airfield boundary. It was the closest most of us had yet been to *legal* low level aerobatics! The memory is still warm of a solo detail wherein Danish Air Force fellow-student Bjorn and I were deliberately doing synchronised circuits – he on the left runway turning left and I on the right runway turning right.

On navigation cross-country trips, the T-bird could climb to over 40,000 feet and cruise happily at Mach .8 (about 500 mph) thanks to a wing design which was to become the basis for the executive Lear jet. The higher speed introduced us to new training problems. For example, the standard aviation rate one turn is 3 degrees per second which changes direction through 180 degrees in one minute. The greater the speed, the more bank is required to achieve the same rate of turn. At Harvard speeds, a rate one turn required about 20 degrees of bank but at 400 knots (460 mph) the bank angle would be closer to 50 degrees, which greatly aggravated the normal aircraft tendency to drop the nose in a turn. Under instrument conditions, high angles of bank made it far too easy to allow the height to vary by alarming amounts.

My instructor watched my early attempts under the hood with increasing impatience as our level varied plus or minus 1,000 feet.

Author with T33a.

Formation close-up.

'I have control!' he announced and peeled the T33 over into a near-vertical dive. Levelling off, he continued,

'You are now 500 feet above Lake Winnipeg. Show me a max rate turn starboard – and now lose 1000 feet!'

The consequent concentration produced an immediate improvement in performance.

However, most exercises were done at around 20,000 feet. Given the distinctive tip fuel tanks, which served the useful additional role of reducing wingtip drag, the average detail could be up to an hour and a half – about double the endurance of a typical British jet. It is also about double the concentration span of the average student, so it was traditional to break off from serious work halfway through and have some fun beating up clouds. This particularly applied during mutual instrument flying practice when one student was required to act as safety pilot 'eyes' for a colleague practising procedures under the hood.

Four plane formation over RCAF Gimli, Manitoba. © RCAF

Author receiving the coveted 'Wings'.

This led to one of the greatest line-shoots (exaggerations) of my career. There was considerable friendly rivalry between the various NATO countries. One pleasant autumn day, I was rostered to act as safety pilot while one of my French fellow students practised radio beacon approaches starting from 20,000 feet. Halfway through, in time-honoured fashion, I said, 'OK, relax – I have control,' and proceeded to have a few minutes of sport aerobatting round the clouds. This indulgence ended with a roll-off-the-top which, by sheer chance, rolled out on the correct heading to the beacon at almost exactly 20,000 feet. My French colleague was mightily impressed, believing (erroneously) that this was a pre-planned manoeuvre. To my shame, I accepted his compliments with a self-deprecating smile, making not the slightest attempt to disillusion him.

The other vivid memory is of a return from a weekend navigation trip with my instructor. As passengers know only too well, there is very little impression of speed in a modern aeroplane because there is no nearby visual reference. On this occasion it was Sunday and the circuit was empty. He received permission for a low pass which took us down the runway at a height of about ten feet and a speed of over 500 knots (580 mph). The overwhelming adrenal surge was cushioned by the fleeting thought that if anything went wrong, I would know very little about it!

The six-month jet conversion flew by and remains in the memory banks as one of the happiest periods of my life. We were living the life of officers but free from any of the responsibilities normally associated with the position – and in seventh heaven at being allowed to play with this wonderful toy. The only flaw was the monastic existence engendered by our remoteness from Winnipeg. Somehow that seemed unimportant as we were already in love – with an aeroplane!

Once again, the multiple choice exams worked in my favour but it was a genuine surprise when I was recommended for a distinguished pass in the course overall and offered a permanent commission in the RCAF if I chose to take it. After my 'Below Average' start in aviation, the T33 had responded to my infatuation by proving to me that I now had the self-confidence to be a pilot. In the meantime, National Service had still to be completed.

With our conspicuously pristine RAF wings shining bright on uniform breasts, we made the long rail trip back to Montreal. The return voyage to Liverpool was courtesy of Cunard and RMS *Carinthia*. December made for a light passenger load but the Atlantic was in a benign mood. We had a pleasant, relaxing week troubled only by speculation about what plans the powers-that-be might have in mind for the remaining nine months of our service.

The answer was soon forthcoming. The RAF was rather snooty about Canadian training being not quite up to scratch (i.e. not the way the RAF did it). The conversion course gave potentially sadistic instructors a golden opportunity to reinforce tribal prejudices about newly fledged RCAF trainees by exposing them to that 'limited panel' instrument flying that the T33's all-singing, all-dancing artificial horizon had made redundant. However, such a course was cost-effective only for those with enough time remaining to be useful to the service. So the good news was that we would not have to do the conversion. The not-so-good news was that we were to be posted to 99 Squadron at Lyneham to be second pilots on Transport Command's Handley Page Hastings.

There was time for a few days at home and a nostalgic visit to the University Air Squadron office in Bute Gardens. I managed to drop a casual reference to the fact that I had come top of a course which included representatives of some of the top universities in the country but the impact was nil. Innes had been regarded as one of the losers and that mindset was destined to continue. However, I had learnt the useful personal lesson that the slow starters are not necessarily always going to be the tortoises.

Transport Command

In the 50s, the Handley Page Hastings was the long-range workhorse of Transport Command. Bizarrely, it was a tail-wheel aeroplane in an aviation world where the tricycle undercarriage had already become the large aeroplane norm. It was rumoured that this was because the army had demanded that the aircraft be able to transport a jeep attached underneath the fuselage. Its civil cousin, the Hermes, had a nose wheel and a brief life with BOAC before being replaced by the more reliable Argonaut. The problem for both Handley Page cousins was that they were powered by four Bristol Hercules radial piston engines. In the air their sleeve valve design and complex electrical harness made for poor reliability. On the ground they had a growling note reminiscent of nothing so much as a quartet of concrete mixers.

*99 Squadron crew with 511 Squadron Hastings at Nicosia. Navigator
(right) paying scant regard to tarmac smoking regulations!*

It is true that the Hastings was required to fill many roles from freighter to dropping paratroops. Although it could carry less than 50 passengers, it required an operating crew of six: two pilots, navigator, flight engineer, wireless operator and loadmaster. The last three were normally senior NCOs while the captain and navigator were usually flight lieutenants. Our role as second pilots was to sit in the right hand seat, raise the undercarriage and flaps on the captain's command and lower them again several hours later.

We were without doubt the lowest form of animal life in the crew. The tail wheel arrangement made the Hastings an absolute pig to land – particularly in crosswinds – and no captain I ever flew with could demonstrate a consistently smooth standard. It followed that the chances of a second pilot being offered a landing were negligible. If the captain visited the loo in the cruise, the navigator would hover suspiciously, making clear his lowly opinion of the competence of the junior colleague.

To be fair, they had good reason for their lack of confidence as the RAF did not think it necessary to provide second pilots with a proper conversion course. All that happened was that another junior who had a few months experience would show us the main cockpit knobs and switches. This briefing was not necessarily comprehensive as I discovered to my extreme embarrassment. My first line trip was from Lyneham to Malta – a journey which took the lumbering beast over six and a half hours. This meant it was already dark as we made our approach. It was my first visit to anywhere in Europe and it coincided with one of the many Maltese festivals. I was fascinated by the spectacle of fireworks bursting all around but my reverie was rudely disturbed when the captain called for landing lights. My confession that I had no idea where the switches were did little to raise the crew's opinion of my usefulness.

Fortunately for second pilot morale, there were smaller aircraft on the station which were available to us with the minimum of fuss. Renewing my acquaintance with the Chipmunk saved my sanity but, more practically, we were also permitted to play with the station Avro Anson. This twin-engine relic of WWII provided a useful introduction to multi-engine operation. Occasionally, there were more exotic treats such as scrounging a ride in the station Gloster Meteor Mk 7 two-seat trainer.

The work pattern of the Hastings did provide some compensation however, by introducing us to foreign climes. My first visit to Cyprus was an eye-opening experience. In those days, RAF aircraft could not overfly the Balkans, so we routed via Malta where RAF Luqa provided a convenient lunch stop. As usual, the captain and navigator were flight lieutenants who, to my youthful eyes, seemed grizzled veterans of the war. In fact, they were probably in their late thirties.

At Luqa we repaired to the officers' mess where I followed the example of my more senior colleagues in sinking a couple of pints to accompany the meal. Duly refreshed, we returned to our aircraft and set off for Cyprus. However grossly irresponsible that may seem in these politically correct times, attitudes to flying and alcohol were much more relaxed in those long-gone days. Some European airlines even served wine to their pilots in flight. Their cultures could not conceive of a meal being complete without it.

Nowadays, the pendulum has over-compensated in that pilot alcohol limits are a quarter of those permitted to car drivers. To put it another way, a young driver in a high-powered car for which he has had no training can be released into the maelstrom of modern traffic with four times the level of alcohol in the blood permitted to a highly-trained airline pilot. This legislation owes much to nameless public suspicion of an industry of which the average layman seems to have little knowledge. In fact there is no known incidence of accidents being attributed to drink in major airlines. This may be because there are two pilots on commercial aircraft and neither has any intention of allowing the other to kill him/her. Also, unlike the roads, the commercial aviation environment is a totally professional one where safety is the prime concern of all involved.

At any rate, we made it safely to Nicosia and were cleared straight in to land in an empty circuit. At the time, EOKA was actively targeting British military personnel as part of its guerrilla war aimed at ending British rule in Cyprus and ultimately creating a union with Greece. The next alarming development was that we were each issued with a loaded revolver together with instructions to have it with us at all times, including keeping it under the pillow at night. Despite the threat, it was decided we would night-stop in a little hotel in town, principally on the grounds that it had an excellent bar and the Wireless Operator had taken a shine to the Austrian widow who ran it. My own misgivings were more to do with the advisability of socialising with an assorted bunch of RAF colleagues carrying loaded weapons than any real fear of shadowy EOKA assassins. The fact that any failure to return the exact number of bullets issued to us would incur a considerable bureaucratic penalty tended to discourage any false heroics.

The hotel proved pleasant enough and a quick change into civvies saw us muster in the aforesaid bar determined on a brave attempt to counter the dreaded effects of airborne dehydration. To our surprise, the sole occupant propping up the counter was another RAF officer -- in Flight Lieutenant's uniform.

'Just arrived?' he inquired, his tone only ever-so-slightly slurred. 'Any problems with Air Traffic Control?'

None at all, we assured him, it had gone very smoothly.

'Jolly good,' he announced, 'I am the duty Air Traffic Controller.'

At the time, my suspicion was that this might have been a leg-pull but many years later I met a steward in British European Airways who had been a Leading Aircraftsman in RAF Nicosia at the time. He was happy to confirm that his boss was in the habit of clearing off to the pub and leaving him in charge of the tower.

While at Lyneham I became the proud owner of my very first motor car. Sadly my relatively impecunious state ruled out the traditional pilot sports car, so my desperate hunger for wheels had to be satisfied by a second hand Standard 8. This was a very basic little four seat saloon – so basic in fact that the boot did not even have an opening lid and could only be accessed from inside the car. Designed to be sold new for £500, it became mine in second hand form for £350. The only shock to mar my burgeoning pride of ownership was that petrol rationing had been re-introduced in Britain as one of the repercussions of Britain's ill-fated attack on Suez in 1956. So for five months in 1957, the miserly ration permitted only a couple of hundred miles a month.

To add insult to injury, we took off from Lyneham one fine day loaded to the gunwales for a long distance trip. We had barely reached cruising altitude when one of the temperamental Hercules engines decided to give up the ghost. As we were well above landing weight for the inevitable return, it became necessary to dump thousands of gallons of prime aviation gasoline over the English countryside. In those innocent days, thoughts of pollution had not yet begun to trouble our

Hastings at Habbaniya, 1957. Crew in tropical kit.

consciences. My imagination merely conjured up a picture of desperate motorists turning their faces to the skies to savour this heavenly dew.

It was another visit to Cyprus which confirmed for me that my youthful impatience was not suited to the tempo of long haul. Once again we routed via Malta but as we approached Luqa, the captain consulted with the flight engineer and decided the lightly-loaded aircraft had enough fuel to carry on non-stop to Nicosia. The eventual flight time was nearly twelve hours and it seemed to me the day would never end as we droned along at less than 10,000 feet. The only advantage of being in an unpressurised aircraft was that you could actually open a cockpit window in flight. The necessary precautions were only brought home to me on the first occasion I tried this when my map vanished out the window and fluttered down into the middle of the wine-dark Mediterranean.

Fortunately, in the presence of a full-time navigator, its only practical value was for my personal enlightenment.

On that particular trip we were bound for RAF Habbaniya in Mesopotamia – the Iraq today. Although the RAF had started building airfields in Jordan with a view to reinforcing our presence in the Middle East, the young King Hussein wanted his country back and these developments were under threat. Our mission was to fly into RAF Mafraq and help in its evacuation. Habbaniya proved to be a green oasis patch by the River Euphrates in an otherwise empty-looking Mesopotamian desert. It even had an open air swimming pool – of which we took full advantage as we waited for further instructions. At night the desert skies gave us a crystal clear view of the Arend-Roland comet's brush with planet Earth.

RAF life could not be all play, however, and a continuation training detail was set up. We were droning happily round the sky practising various procedures when the skipper swore loudly, closed the throttles and started a rapid descent. In response to my startled enquiry as to the nature of his alarm, he gestured towards the eastern horizon, which had disappeared in a yellow haze. As we expedited onto a final approach to Habbaniya, the forward visibility was dropping sharply and by the time we taxied in it had reduced further to a few hundred yards in flying sand. It was my first experience of a desert sandstorm and there was little doubt that, had our approach been a few minutes later, Habbaniya would have been closed to us.

Eventually, however, orders came for us to proceed to Mafraq in Jordan where, in stark contrast to Habbaniya's dusty tarmac, we landed on an immaculate, brand-new 3,000 metre runway, built to the RAF's very latest standards. Mafraq was to be one of the new airfields to police the Middle East. One of the most common problems in a new airfield was a lack of married quarters for families. In Mafraq this had been rectified in spades – the only buildings erected so far were married quarters! Station Head Quarters and the Officer's Mess were both in domestic buildings.

The point of our mission was highlighted by the fact that Jordanian tanks could be seen in the distance around the airfield. But any 'relief of Mafeking' pride we might have had was swiftly dashed when we discovered that our return load was to be twelve tons of unserviceable wireless equipment to be taken back to Britain to be written off. It may have been top secret kit useful to an enemy but, if so, we were not told. Such absurdities at the tax-payers expense bedevilled the service at the time – and possibly still do.

British European Airways

s the end of our National Service loomed, the prospects for finding gainful employment were the subject of much debate in the mess. Fortunately, an explosion in commercial air transport was about to begin and both British Overseas Airways Corporation (BOAC) and British European Airways Corporation (BEA) were advertising for pilots. BOAC with its intercontinental network was the clear winner in the glamour stakes but my dearest wish was to fly in Scotland. It was bad enough that new second officers in BOAC would have to spend a year or more acting as navigators but, on top of that, Transport Command had already proven I was constitutionally unsuited to long-haul flying.

So BEA was the main target of my efforts. When summoned for interview, my colleague, Eric Green and I felt we had played a trump card when we arranged a training cross-country exercise in the station Anson from Lyneham to Northolt, then the location of BEA headquarters. It seemed a very practical use of the last flight of my National Service. Our interviews were chaired by BEA's Flight Operations Director, Captain Bill Baillie. As chief pilot of Scottish Airways during the war years, he had operated the first Dakota flights between Glasgow and Northolt in November 1946. Whether our particular piece of initiative influenced the interviewing panel or not it is impossible to say, but we were both accepted. Neither of us had the essential civil licences but the airlines were so conscious of the need for pilots that we were offered an unbeatable deal. Not only would BEA employ us at the princely salary of £10 a week while we studied for the commercial exams but would also

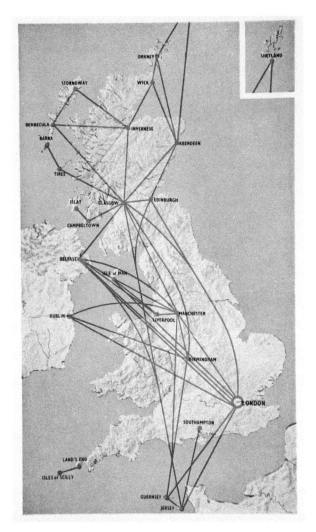

BEA domestic network, 1959.

train us to fly their workhorse Dakotas – including the vital Instrument Rating essential for all commercial operations in cloud.

So in September 1957, I checked out of RAF Lyneham, had a few days leave in South Uist and two days later joined BEA in London. £10 a week might have been worth a lot more in those days but it did not permit such luxuries as car ownership while paying for digs in Hounslow. Sadly, my Standard 8 had to go.

BEA's Viking Training Centre of the time was located just under the glide path of London Airport's main south runway – then known as 28 Left from its compass heading of 278 degrees. There we mixed with future career-long colleagues, including the sophisticated ones with much more jet time than us who were destined to go straight on to the Viscount 700. In the classroom, we lesser mortals were introduced to the technical mysteries of the Dakota by 'Pop' Speller – a splendid old expert in the eccentricities of Air Registration Board exams. These aircraft exams, essential to having the type added to our pilot licences, were set by engineers. This meant we were required to absorb much information about such esoteric items as the turnbuckles, which adjusted the control cables under the floor. These fascinating details were deemed somewhat academic by pilots who did not much care how said cables were adjusted so long as the flying surfaces responded correctly when we waggled the control column.

More appropriately, the basic Commercial Pilot's Licence required us to study for the wide range of subjects that were actually related to our future role such as Navigation, Meteorology, Flight Planning and Air Law. Even more practical was that basic forerunner of the sophisticated flight simulators of today: the Link Trainer. Within that primitive box we learnt the pilot-interpreted approach procedures of civil aviation, while our apprentice tracks were drawn on a map for all to see by a device which crawled about on a table like some Heath Robinson crab.

One by one, the hurdles were surmounted and in December 1957 we found ourselves on the fun bit of any conversion course – the chance to play with the real aeroplane for the first time without the potential embarrassment of passengers. Jersey was one of BEA's bases with an off-season lightness of traffic which made it eminently suitable for the purpose. The fact that it was also an engineering base was to prove useful.

Thousands of DC3/C47/Dakota aircraft had become surplus at the end of the war - sometimes for prices as low as $1.00! They were now the workhorses of short

Forerunner of the super-sophisticated simulators of today, the Link Trainer as museum piece at the headquarters of Northwest Airlines (now part of Delta) in Minnesota-St Paul. The 'crab' which recorded the student's apprentice efforts can be seen bottom right.

Pionairs at the Jersey engineering base, 1957.

haul aviation. BEA had removed the wireless operator's station and substituted an extra row of seats together with an air-stair in the passenger door. The resultant 32-seater was known in the airline as the 'Pionair', recognisable in old pictures by having eight windows per side rather than the standard seven.

The original C47 had been designed to be flown from the left-hand seat with the assistance of a relatively inexperienced second pilot on the right. The only flying instruments were on the left panel, so any co-pilot lucky enough to be given a sector to fly would have to switch seats. This practice ignored the fundamental part that muscle memory plays in any manual skill and the consequent unfamiliarity was deemed to have played a part in more than one accident. Some airlines had a compromise modification whereby the main flying instrument panel was placed in the centre behind the throttles. BEA's policy was to have fully-qualified First Officers, so the Pionair had a second instrument flying panel fitted on the right with the autopilot control instruments in the centre.

The Harvard had been powered by a Pratt and Whitney radial engine driving a Hamilton propeller so that experience at last proved its worth as an invaluable preparation for dealing with the Dakota's more powerful versions, Few modern jet or turboprop passengers will have experienced the engine run-up ceremony prior to entering the runway which was de rigueur on piston-engined aircraft. Several minutes passed as propeller pitch controls were exercised and the dual magnetos were checked at various power settings. The consequent variation in engine noise levels can have done little for the morale of nervous passengers unaware that this was all in the interest of their continuing well-being. In flight oil temperatures and pressures usually gave the first warning of possible trouble and therefore had to be continually monitored. Temperatures could be adjusted by opening gill-like louvres on the engine casings which increased ventilation air through the engines.

Jersey in winter, with just a handful of services a day, was a suitably quiet and remote airfield to come to grips with landing this classic tail-dragger. We flew in pairs with a training captain, taking turns to attempt the various exercises. Time on the jump seat was not wasted for we found that there was much to be learnt from watching a colleague's mistakes and triumphs.

Jersey echoed to the sonorous roar of Dakota propellers as we eventually got back in the air and pounded our way round the circuit. We soon grasped the basic technique of wheeling the old lady onto the runway but the course was enlivened by one piece of drama when one of the other training crews attempted a take-off. As they rolled down the westerly runway 27, the port propeller parted company with its engine. As a result, the Dakota swung off the runway in a gentle arc and came to rest in front of the control tower. With commendable coolness, Captain Pigden pressed the transmit button and said,

'As you can see, Tower, we are unable to taxi. Request assistance!'

When the incident was analysed, my friend Eric realised just how lucky he had been. His jump seat was just behind the captain on the left, slightly forward of the defective propeller. This was a known dangerous place to be in a wheels-up Dakota emergency landing because of the risk of the port propeller penetrating the fuselage. On this occasion, the offending item had departed downwards, struck the runway *underneath* the aeroplane and spun away on the right-hand side. It was pure luck that it had not come straight through the side of the fuselage by his seat.

On the social side, we found that the entertainment at our hotel attracted some eye-catching local talent who seemed not at all averse to fraternising with future airline pilots. The Scots amongst us celebrated New Year's Eve 1958 with particular zest, failing to appreciate we were now in a 24/365 business. We struggled with our New Year's Day training detail in a somewhat fragile condition, looking for early relief as the evening gloom gathered on the short winter's day. Imagine the silent dismay when the training captain announced,

'I feel good. We might as well get the night flying out of the way!'

One by one, the various boxes on the forms were ticked off. It was a particular relief that we were able to pass the test for the Instrument Rating (essential for

Anorak point: the BEA Pionair can be recognised by its eight passenger windows rather than the C47's usual seven. BEA had removed the wireless operator's station and fitted an extra row of seats to bring the potential passenger load to 32. Elsan equipped loo at the rear. © BA

commercial operation in cloud) within the relatively friendly environment of the aircraft we were to use. The alternative would have been an expensive visit to the Civil Aviation examining unit at Stansted, which had acquired a reputation for nit-picking criticism which filled all would-be airline pilots with nameless dread. We considered ourselves fortunate indeed that BEA had dispensation to carry out its own testing on the aeroplane we were to fly. Eventually, we became the proud possessors of commercial licences, which testified that we were deemed fit to carry passengers on C47a type aeroplanes.

Little did we realise how much we still had to learn!

Scotland's forgotten airport

It would seem that the modern highway designer has an inbuilt horror of straight lines. Whether it be for reasons of alleviating boredom or restricting speeding temptations, it is rare in Britain to encounter a stretch of modern roadway free from continuous curves. In carving its way through the heart of the Glasgow sprawl, the westbound M8 is a fine example of this philosophy save for one stretch. Immediately after the exit to the mammoth Braehead shopping paradise, the carriageway runs straight as an arrow for over a mile. Presumably only elderly travellers are nowadays aware that they owe this rare planning aberration to the fact that the road follows

The futuristic terminal building at Renfrew Airport as seen from the staff car park in 1959. A couple of Pionairs are visible far left.

the line of what was once the main 26/08 runway at Renfrew aerodrome, Glasgow's airport until the mid-sixties. Its proximity to the current Glasgow International (Abbotsinch) explains why the two were sometimes confused in the past. Renfrew airport's first incarnation had been as Moorpark Aerodrome on the lands of Newmains farm. During WWI it was used by the Royal Flying Corps and for acceptance flying of the aircraft being produced by Scottish factories.

Despite the R34's pioneer 1919 Atlantic crossing, civil aviation progress in Scotland was slow in the 1920s (see Appendix 1), although some survivors of the air war turned to flying circuses and joyride flying to eke out a living. In the 1930s, the picture changed. Domestic air services came to the Highlands and Islands of Scotland long before there was any real demand for them on the rest of the country. The cruising speed of passenger aircraft in the thirties was not much more than 100 mph (and speed over the ground could be considerably reduced with headwinds). This offered little challenge to the comprehensive steam train network of pre-WWII Britain.

Where sea crossings were involved the equation became quite different. When it might take two days to travel from Glasgow to the Outer Hebrides by surface transport, a potential flying time of less than two hours had obvious attraction. The first scheduled air services in Scotland were operated by Midland and Scottish Air Ferries from Renfrew to Campbeltown and Islay in April 1933. On 14 May of that year, Captain Jimmy Orrell flew his DH Dragon on the first ambulance flight to collect a sick fisherman from Islay. Eight days later, on 22 May, his second mercy flight was to Clachan sands in North Uist to bring home the terminally ill Reverend Malcolm Gillies. The potential importance of air ambulance flights to remote islands was clear. In June, Jimmy toured the Western Isles searching for likely landing sites and selected, amongst others, the machair at Sollas, North Uist.

MSAF deserve also to be remembered for employing the petite figure of the redoubtable Winnie Drinkwater. She earned her commercial licence before her twentieth birthday, thereby becoming not just the youngest female commercial pilot but arguably the youngest commercial pilot in the world. Not only did she fly some of the first Scottish passenger services to the islands but she also qualified as an aircraft engineer! Sadly for the diversity of aviation, her career was far too brief. It was while tinkering with the innards of an engine in greasy overalls that she was spotted by Francis Short, a director of the famous Belfast firm, Short Brothers. Apparently he fell for her 'head over heels' and they married in July 1934.

In Inverness, larger-than-life character Ted Fresson made it his mission to open up services to the Orkneys and Shetlands. Operating basic aircraft in an area

A crowd welcomes the first ambulance flight to North Uist in 1933. Ina Ferguson, the little three-year-old girl (in white hat left of centre) would one day become an air ambulance nurse.

with atrocious weather and an absence of modern navigational aids, his Highland Airways achieved the astonishing record of operating at 98% regularity in the three years before the war. He claimed his pilots could operate primitive deHavilland Dragon biplanes in winds of up to 70 knots (80 mph). The technique was to fly the aeroplane onto the ground, maintaining the flying attitude with engines running while up to a dozen handlers stopped it from taking off again until a suitably sturdy vehicle could be lashed to the tail. The subsequent departure would be as vertical as any helicopter! Fresson was awarded the first Air Mail contract in Britain between Inverness and Orkney. He had hoped to open a base in Aberdeen but Gandar Dower's Aberdeen Airways secured the better field at Dyce Farm (which gave its name to the modern Aberdeen airport).

Post-war, these small specialised airlines fell victim to the new Labour Government's love of nationalisation. Long haul intercontinental services were to be the hunting ground of British Overseas Airways Corporation while European and domestic routes were to be the province of British European Airways. Officially, the latter came into being on 1 August 1946 as a crown corporation. Initially, it was established as two divisions: Northolt for continental flights and Liverpool Speke for domestic schedules. For a time Railway Air Services at Liverpool continued to operate flights between London and Scotland in conjunction with Scottish Airways. From the previously independent constituent parts the new corporation inherited a motley collection of aircraft. These included a couple of Dakotas and thirteen Avro Ansons plus eight Junkers 52s accepted from Germany as war reparations.

Unfortunately, the latter (and their engines) had been built in anticipation of the very short life of wartime aircraft. The slow and lumbering Ju52's corrugated metal skin did little to inspire confidence in aerodynamic efficiency. Indeed, Captain Bill St. Clair Reid argued it was the only aeroplane he ever flew which had its performance improved when ice picked up in flight smoothed out the wrinkles! The third engine mounted in the nose created its own problems. Not only did it give rise to considerable noise, fumes and vibration in the cockpit but also ensured that the Ju52 suffered from the same problems as a single-engined aircraft in terms of the obstruction of forward visibility while taxiing. Some pilots hit on a novel solution, making use of the hatch in the cockpit roof. They simply stood on the seat with head and shoulders out of the hatch – for all the world like wartime tank commanders.

Junkers Ju52 at Sumburgh. (BEA designation - Jupiter)

The deHavilland 89 Rapide. © BA

The brakes were powered by air bottles which had a habit of expiring at inconvenient moments. Originally, the brakes had been powered by air from engine compressors but BEA engineers in their wisdom decided to dispense with these. Unfortunately, a multi-sector day away from the main base could completely exhaust the supply, creating obvious difficulties for the pilot. In the end, reliability was so poor that the Ju52s were withdrawn from service within the year.

The bulk of the initial fleet consisted of forty seven De Havilland Dragon Rapide biplanes. Some of these had been the mainstay of the various Scottish services and merely continued in that role under their new owner.

Graceful little aeroplane though the Rapide was, it was also a 30s design, primitive by today's standards. Basically a wooden framework covered in doped fabric, it could carry six or seven passengers in such close proximity that someone seated on the left could easily touch the right-hand side. It was crewed by a single pilot and a radio officer. Before radio telephony replaced Morse code wireless telephony, the latter was responsible for communications and obtaining the homing bearings essential in bad weather letdowns.

Two Gipsy Queen engines gave a reasonable short field performance but the cruise speed was only about 100 knots (115 mph). Payload was so restricted that it was necessary to weigh the passengers as well as their luggage and every attempt was made not to roster two large crew members together. Fully laden, the Rapide was unlikely to be able to maintain altitude if an engine failed so trust had to be placed in the belief that ground effect (an improved performance given by close proximity to the surface) would save the aircraft from actual contact with terra firma!. Clearly this was of little comfort on mountain transits.

Rapides operated some of the early services between Croydon and Glasgow but headwinds often reduced the groundspeed and required a re-fuelling stop on the northerly journey. As indicated earlier, they offered little competition to the faster and more comfortable intercity trains of the 30s. But where water crossings were involved, the Rapide came into its own.

Its most significant shortcoming when it came to Scottish winter operations was that there was no provision for anti-icing or de-icing. Given that temperature falls by approximately two degrees Celsius per 1,000 feet of climb, any aircraft operating in the cold, soggy clouds which sweep across Britain in the winter can expect to have ice form on the flying surfaces with a consequent serious effect on performance. The Rapide's wings, braces and struts made excellent ice-gathering devices and the only protection plan was to spread grease on leading edges in the hope of providing a less hospitable surface.

The problem is clearly illustrated by a 1937 report from Captain Eric Lane-Burslem who was flying the Rapide's big sister – the four-engined DH86 – from Budapest back to London. He was forced to enter cloud at 9,000 feet over Germany:

'In quick succession the struts, wires and wings iced up. We tried in vain to get bearings using the fixed aerial until that broke off and of course the blind flying instruments were running down.

My efforts to trim the ice-laden aircraft were not helped by the loss of engine power. And then they stopped... port outer, starboard outer, followed by both inners. We were descending over the Taunus Mountains and I was waiting for the bump. Instead we broke cloud at about 5,000 feet to find ourselves in a valley. The engines came back to life; we trailed a spare aerial, fixed our position and made a safe landing in Nuremburg!'

North of Glasgow, letdown aids for Scottish airports were few and far between. Small wonder that pilots were reluctant to enter cloud in winter time if it could be avoided. Some ingenious low level routes were devised. From the Hebrides, you could run down between Mull and Iona, turn left through the Corryvreckan Strait between Sgarba and Jura, cross Kintyre *through* the Crinan Canal, continue via Loch Fyne, the Kyles of Bute and the Clyde to Renfrew.

Captain Harry MacDowell used that particular route once from Tiree to Glasgow without exceeding 200 feet at any stage of the flight. As he left the aeroplane at Glasgow he found two gentlemen still standing on the tarmac awaiting his arrival.

'Captain,' said one, 'thank you for a wonderful flight. Not really very much like flying, though. More like being on a high speed boat!'

Another useful low level alternative was from Inverness to Stornoway. By dint of following the A835 it was possible to route through the mountains without exceeding 1,000 feet. In strong winds, however, this would be ruled out by the unacceptable level of turbulence generated by the terrain.

Anecdotes from the Rapide era were many and varied. Captain Benny Yorston landed at Tiree one day to find he had an engine problem. There were only three passengers for Glasgow, Lord and Lady ****** and their daughter, an elegant lady in her twenties. He explained to them that there was no engineer cover at Tiree so they would have to wait for another aeroplane to arrive from Glasgow with the appropriate specialist. At this point the daughter spoke up.

'Well, do you know, Captain, I served in the Wrens during the war. Did a lot of work on Dominies (the military designation of the Rapide). Could I have a look?'

Thinking there was nothing to lose, Benny agreed. She fiddled around under the cowlings and very shortly declared the problem solved. Having inspected her solution, Benny felt able to sign the aircraft Technical Log in approval and back to Glasgow they flew. After all, there is nothing more comforting to a pilot than having an engineer confident enough in his/her handiwork to actually board the flight!

You might not think that this could happen nowadays, in an age of advanced technology and even more advanced bureaucracy. However, I did once find myself stuck on the Greek island of Zakinthos with a problem on a Boeing 757. I informed the passengers of our plight while pondering gloomily the chances of finding accommodation at short notice for over two hundred and thirty passengers on a small island. As if by magic, it transpired that amongst the holidaying passengers was one of our own engineers, appropriately licensed to deal with our problem. Fate truly smiled upon us on that occasion.

Given the lack of navigation aids in Scotland post-war, pilots relied heavily on old-fashioned map reading and local knowledge. In the absence of radar, air traffic control was largely procedural. Regardless of weather, modern commercial flights are almost invariably flown under Instrument Flight Rules whereby the traffic is regulated and separated by Air Traffic Control. In 50s Scotland, instrument flight plans were often cancelled and sometimes never even filed. It was often more efficient to remain below cloud and be responsible for one's own separation from the light traffic of the time than climb into the murk and be faced with a long-winded, non-precision procedural approach at the other end without any guarantee of a successful outcome.

There could be traps, however. One of the Rapide schedules alternated between Campbeltown and Islay. It was a very pleasant route on a fine summer's day so Jimmy Scotland was quite happy to proceed under Visual Flight Rules. It was only passing Largs that he realised that, in the absence of a flight plan, he could not remember whether he was bound for Campbeltown or Islay. Turning to his trusty Radio Officer, he asked,

'Where are we landing?'

'I thought you knew,' was the less-than-helpful reply.

Fortunately, the R/O was a man of ready wit. Turning to the only passengers (easy to do in the intimacy of the Rapide) he enquired casually, 'Going on holiday, sir?'

'No, we live on Islay' came the useful response.

'Islay!' he hissed to his captain and blushes were spared.

Ailsa Cousins about to board a BEA Rapide for the Scilly Isles. © Bruce Cousins

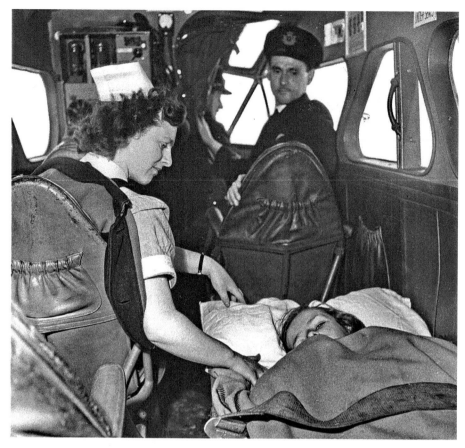

Rapide ambulance flight with sister from the Southern General. The Radio Officer's wireless station can be seen on the cockpit bulkhead. © *British Airways*

The Islay route was popular with local farmers, often accompanied by their trusty collies. At Renfrew, one particularly large specimen of the breed was loaded in his box into the Rapide's small hold behind the passenger cabin. On the way to Islay, the pilot started experiencing some very strange difficulties with the control of his aircraft. The mystery was solved on arrival at Islay. It transpired that the dog had escaped from his crate and gnawed a hole in the side of the hold. When the aeroplane was seen on final approach into Islay, the faithful hound was sitting with his head out of the side of the fuselage, ears pinned back by the blast, contentedly admiring the scene while completely oblivious of the effect his disruption of the airflow was having on elevators and rudder just behind. The simplicity of the Rapide construction saved the day for the return flight. A patch was slapped over the hole, dope was applied and the integrity of the airframe was restored!

BEA Renfrew

Today there is little to remind the thousands of motorists using the M8 that there ever was an airport at Renfrew. However, if westbound travellers look to their left, they can still see the cemetery which rather ominously dominated the view for the departing air passenger. When it was replaced as Glasgow's airport by the move to Abbotsinch, the once-futuristic airport buildings made way for a council estate. How many of its current residents know why their roads have names like Viscount Way and Heron Way?

In 1958, Renfrew was still BEA's main base in Scotland. As the majority of the airline's pilots were English, it was considered by most an unpopular posting to be endured only by those co-pilots and captains too junior to bid for bases closer to home. BEA had other bases at Manchester, Jersey and Aberdeen but London Airport (now Heathrow) was the centre of the airline's world and therefore the most attractive to the ambitious career pilot. It was a great relief for the Personnel Department when people like me actually volunteered to go to Glasgow. I was very keen to fly around my own country and it was only much later that I realised that I had fortuitously stumbled into one of the finest aviation training environments in the world.

BEA Renfrew still had many of the pre-war pioneers who had played major roles in setting up the air routes of Scotland between the wars. Flight Manager

View from the Renfrew control tower. An Avro York mixes with the BEA types. The chimney on the right served as a useful visual marker for the threshold of Runway 21.

Scotland was Eric Starling, who had been chief pilot for Gandar Dower's operation from Aberdeen to the Northern Isles. David Barclay was already a legend in the air ambulance service. He had been chief pilot of Scottish Airways at Renfrew before its absorption into BEA and had pioneered aviation services to the Western Isles. An accident on a wartime flight had left him with a slight limp with one leg too weak to cope with the rudder inputs required for single-engine flight on the Dakota. His flying was therefore confined to the deHavilland Heron, which was used for the Tiree/Barra service and ambulance flights. Promotion to captain in BEA was by seniority in the airline and Renfrew as a posting was even less popular with first command English-based pilots who had already acquired a home in the south. If forced to move to Renfrew they were only too happy to escape to pastures warmer as soon as a vacancy existed. It followed that many of the line captains were new commands and many of the co-pilots were on their first posting within the airline. The consequent considerable turnover of personnel entailed a heavy training programme. Winter, being the season of least commercial demand, is the normal airline training season. Given the dramatic variations of the Scottish winter, the Renfrew training programme was a testing one for both learners and training captains. Fortunately, the latter were more than equal to the task. Most of them were happily domiciled Scots who knew the Highland routes like the proverbial back-of-the-hand. To my 24-year-old eyes they seemed just as ancient and wise as my RAF captains had been, but in fact most were still in their late thirties and had accumulated thousands of hours on C47s in wartime. Most of my training was conducted by Harry MacDowell (who had been with Scottish Airways before BEA), Jimmy Scotland and Bill Mackenzie.

The day after my final check in Jersey, I found myself in the admin office in the futuristic-looking Renfrew terminal building. Running the

Author in Second Officer's winter uniform

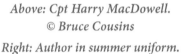

Above: Cpt Harry MacDowell.
© Bruce Cousins
Right: Author in summer uniform.

office (and therefore my future working life) was affable ex-Radio Officer Jimmy Mitchell with the assistance of secretary Margaret Coupar.

Accommodation, as my first priority, was easily dealt with. Mrs Spalter's Victorian villa at 32 St. Andrews Drive in Pollokshields had become a haven for transient BEA pilots. (The building still stands but is now a Sikh temple).

Resplendent in my new uniform with its single stripe, I had time for the briefest of flying visits home to Uist. Riding shotgun on the Benbecula service gave an intriguing foretaste of what was to come. As a newly-qualified Second Officer my salary had doubled from £10 a week to over £1000 per annum. These figures may seem like petty cash to modern aviators but the salary was already more than the £900 I might have achieved after 18 years in my original career choice as a graduate teacher.

On 26 January 1958, I reported for my first training trip with real live commercial passengers. The excitement was intense as I climbed into the Pionair, inhaling its unique aroma: a mixture of leather, hydraulic fluid and aviation gasoline. Harry MacDowell was charged with my initiation into the art of the co-pilot but fortunately that first trip presented minimal navigation problems during an easy half-hour each way return to Belfast's old airport at Nutts Corner. Short flights to destinations such as Campbeltown and Islay were the pattern for the next few days as I got used to Scottish air traffic procedures and basic co-pilot duties.

The latter were in a state of flux. Many airlines and their pilots have always had a conservative approach to operation procedures, taking the line that there was no need to change established custom and practice. BEA realised early that their war-time generation captains might have established individual habits of varying eccentricity, therefore requiring co-pilots to display considerable psychology and diplomacy skills. Even on multi-crew aircraft the handling pilot often expected to operate as a one-man band while the rest of the crew looked on admiringly. Much of the time, that worked perfectly satisfactorily but in bad weather with primitive aids the handling pilot's workload could escalate alarmingly, particularly in the approach phase. In fog in particular it was recognised that the transition from instrument flying to visual cues close to the ground was a phase fraught with potential for error. The shortness of the visual segment available at the end of a successful approach tended to generate an instinctive urge to lower the nose in a fruitless but possibly dangerous attempt to improve the view, thus risking premature ground contact.

BEA was always an innovative airline, willing to experiment with procedures. Their main operational difficulty in Europe was fog or, to be more precise in an era which relied so much on coal fires, smog. In Glasgow, winter pea-souper smog might set in for a week or more, reducing visibility to a few yards and rendering air travel impossible. In those days, before central heating became commonplace, I remember seeing the visibility *inside* one of the many huge Glasgow cinemas reduced by vestiges of the smog outside. More strategically important for BEA, the main hub at London Heathrow was also vulnerable and any disruption there created problems for the entire network in terms of diverted aircraft and crews out of position.

Early autopilots were capable of fairly simple tasks like maintaining height and heading but of limited use in bad weather approaches. BEA decided that the future required an automatic system capable of landing the aircraft when there was little or no visual reference. This was to be a key design parameter for the projected jets of the future. In the meantime, it was recognised that in a manual approach the workload for a captain might well reduce his overall situational awareness and that the greatest scope for error was the transition from instrument flight to visual landing. (It remains so to this day for one-man-band pilots at airfields with few landing aids).

Given that they were now recruiting a very high standard of co-pilot from the services, BEA opted for a team operation In limiting conditions the co-pilot would fly the approach down to the decision height for the procedure in use.

The captain would then be left free to monitor the situation, liaise with air traffic control regarding any changes to conditions and be able to make sure of his visual references before taking control for the landing. In the event of the captain deciding there was insufficient visual reference at the height limit on the day, the co-pilot (having remained on instruments throughout) would continue smoothly into the overshoot procedure without any interruption to his instrument scan. This teamwork approach to the job was deemed to make best use of each pilot's skills. On the whole, the younger co-pilots were more familiar with the new-fangled Instrument Landing Systems now available at the bigger airports while the captain would be allowed more thinking time to apply his superior experience to the supervision of the operation.

This so-called 'monitored approach' was considered revolutionary at the time, some believing that it challenged the captain's authority and control of his aircraft. BEA stressed that, on the contrary, it emphasised the management aspects of the captain's role. The captain was still in charge and was more likely to be critical of any shortcomings than if the positions were reversed. It was an era when there was more respect for authority than is currently fashionable.

However, there were many objectors, not least in our sister long-haul airline BOAC, notorious for resistance to change. In the late 60s one of their captains actually wrote to *Flight International* that he saw no reason to change the procedures he had been taught in the RAF twenty five years before. This overlooked two fundamental points:

a) Aviation had changed in the intervening twenty five years.

b) In the meantime, the RAF had also adopted the monitored approach.

There was more to come. The general custom in aviation of the time was to memorise checklists and many retired pilots can still rattle off the basic take-off and landing checks of their first aircraft. With the increasing complexity and sophistication of the ever-changing fleet, BEA decided that checklists would be printed in detail and read out on a challenge and response basis to make sure that nothing was missed. In general there was to be much more emphasis on a standard operating procedure so that there would be less need for co-pilots to adjust to individual commander eccentricities. (It is interesting to note that it took over fifty years for the medical profession to realise that similar checklists might have a significant effect on death rates in the operating theatre).

Whatever their personal views might have been on these mandates from on high, my training captains did their best to train me in these novel ideas.

There was another aspect of weather which posed greater problems in Scotland than anywhere else on the network – the strength of the wind. Winds of sixty or eighty miles an hour are not uncommon in the Hebrides and gales have frequently been known to exceed 100 mph. The slower the aircraft, the greater the problems such winds posed on take-off or landing. Tailwheel machines like the DC3 had further complications even while taxiing on the ground. Unlike the modern 'tricycle' airliners with a nose wheel, tailwheel aircraft have an inbuilt tendency to weathercock into wind, as I had discovered on the Chipmunk. Even when the wind was straight down the runway, taxiing to or from the ramp could become very difficult. Apart from the aeroplane doing its best to turn into wind, turning down wind might allow a strong gale to lift the tail and cause a nose-over. To deal with these problems on the ground, pilots of tail-draggers were accustomed to hold aileron into a cross wind and (counter-intuitively) push the stick forward to deflect the elevators downward when the wind was astern. On the DC3, the relatively primitive autopilot was pressed into service to assist in the process so that the pilot did not have to maintain a control column input.

Earlier aircraft like the Rapide, being much lighter and with lower stalling speeds than the Dakota, were even more vulnerable. There were occasions when the wind strength might gust above their minimum flying speed. When pilots decided that a medical emergency warranted an ambulance flight in extreme conditions, it was customary for two sturdy firemen to grab the wing tips on landing and then climb onto the wings, one on each side, to prevent the machine becoming inadvertently airborne again!

Fireman Donald Macphee in Benbecula reminisced to me about one such occasion when David Barclay landed in a howling gale to pick up a patient.

'You hung on to a strut,' he said, 'with the propeller whizzing round just in front of your face.'

With the ambulance providing some shelter on the ramp, the patient was safely loaded on board. As David started up, the firemen climbed back on to the wings for the taxi out.

'He turned into wind, opened the cockpit window and shouted to us to jump off. As we fellbackwards off the wings, the Rapide went up like a helicopter!'

'They wouldn't do it now,' I ventured.

'Too right,' he laughed, 'with Health and Safety nowadays, you need to put your helmet on to go to the toilet!'

On the Dakota, while taxiing was difficult enough in strong winds, crosswind take-offs and landings were potentially even more fraught. On take-off, the tendency to swing into wind was countered by differential thrust until the rudder started to bite. Directional control had to be assured before raising the tail into the flying attitude as the gyroscopic effect of changing the plane of the propellers could induce a further swing.

Landings were trickier still. Technically, the permitted crosswind component for the Dakota was 18 knots (21 mph) but that would have been prohibitively limiting in the wind speeds regularly encountered in the Highlands and Islands. The Kick-Off-Drift-at-the-Last-Moment method beloved of the RAF had to be discarded as totally inadequate. Instead, a bit of into-wind aileron was fed in on short finals and the subsequent bank reduced by use of opposite rudder. The aeroplane was now in a controlled sideslip and continued in this state to be wheeled onto the runway with the touchdown initially favouring the upwind main wheel. The tail was lowered gradually to maintain rudder control as long as possible and then differential brake

A BEA Pionair departs Renfrew for the Hebrides while a Heron arrives in the background. (Painting by Dugald Cameron in the author's collection.)

could be used to maintain directional control. Meanwhile, the non-handling pilot would whip the flaps up on touchdown to discourage any unwanted tendency to part company with terra firma in gusts. This was an early anticipation of the modern jet's lift dump system whereby the airbrakes on the wing go to maximum deflection on touchdown.

Most Highland airfields were ex-RAF and therefore blessed with at least three runways, giving a total of six potential landing directions. Even that provision (generous by today's standards) was not enough to cater for the capricious versatility of the Scottish gales. Recognising that the recommended technique was not instinctive, our line training concentrated on drilling us to an acceptable level of skill. To this end, it helped that there was virtually no formal air traffic control at the peripheral airfields north and west of Glasgow. Instead, the old RAF fields provided a homing facility and an Air Information Service on weather and runway conditions. The choice of landing direction was left to the pilot, who would normally choose the runway most closely aligned with the wind. During line training, however, Harry would invariably select whichever runway was at right angles to the wind. By the end of my time with him, I was so used to crabbing down the approach path that it felt distinctly odd when light winds allowed the nose to actually point at the touchdown area.

A few months after I had been cleared for line flying, I was rostered with Harry for a Hebridean trip, which for him was a rare non-training day. Stornoway reported their wind as 190 degrees at 20 knots (23 mph). 'We'll land on runway 19,' said my captain in his distinctive tones. There was a moment's stunned silence on the radio followed by the surprised comment, 'But that's into wind!'

A good training captain has to allow the trainee to experience as much of the performance envelope as can be safely arranged. It follows that the supervisor must be confident in his/her own ability to retrieve the situation if the trainee fails to cope. Kirkwall airport was another ex-military field with the usual three runway set-up. The shortest was 33 (now 32). At the time it was about 900 metres long complicated by a 1 in 50 down slope which ended in the water of the bay. There was nothing in the way of approach guidance and the terrain also sloped towards the threshold (which is notorious for giving the pilot false visual cues). However, Harry felt it presented an excellent opportunity for me to practice short field technique. Although the Dakota's normal approach speed was 90 knots, he briefed me to reduce that to 75 knots approaching the airfield boundary. Trusting in my training captain, I obediently did as he suggested and the landing passed off without incident. The reaction of the station superintendent was more dramatic.

Services from Glasgow and Aberdeen at Kirkwall, 1959.

'You b****r,' was his less-than-fraternal greeting to Harry. 'You made him do that landing. I've had *captains* divert rather than use that runway!'

Even when the wind was straight down the runway, there were days when the power of the Scottish gales might mean that taxiing was difficult if not impossible. The solution was simple. The Dakota would stop on the runway and joining passengers were brought out by a bus which would park in front of the aircraft to provide some shelter. Once everyone was safely on board and the bus had left with the arrivals, full flap was lowered, brakes were released and the wind was allowed to blow the aircraft back down the runway to the take-off position! With a castoring tail wheel it was by no means easy to keep straight but the brakes and the engines gave sufficient control. In any case, the strength of the wind ensured that the full length of the runway was rarely necessary. By such means the services could continue in winds up to sixty miles an hour – more than the Dakota's minimum flying speed!

The robustness of the old lady had been the saviour of many an airman during the war. It is well illustrated by an amazing incident that occurred on 14 December 1946. When BEA was formally established as a crown corporation on 1 August earlier that year, its services between Northolt and Scotland were operated initially by Railway Air Services in conjunction with Scottish Airways.

On the day in question, Dakota G-AWZA was due to depart for Glasgow under the command of Captain W.J. Johnson with co-pilot 'Bing' Crosby, Radio Officer Hugh Murdoch and Scottish Airways' first Stewardess, Robina 'Bobbie' Christie. Blizzard conditions had halted landings and discouraged all passengers except for a staff member, John Livingstone, who had work awaiting him in Glasgow. Although the aircraft had been cleared of snow and ice, there was a further temperature drop as they taxied out and a delay to the take-off allowed more snow to freeze on the wings. Departure was to the east and it rapidly became obvious that ZA was struggling to gain height. Its port wing hit the roof of a new semi-detached house and it swung to the left to come to rest perched precariously on the remains of the roof of the neighbouring 46 Angus Drive.

When the stewardess and the radio officer moved to the rear in an attempt to open the passenger door, ZA began to tip. That plan was hurriedly abandoned and they exited instead through the emergency windows over the wing. From there they made their way through the wreckage of the loft down the stairs and out through the front door! Amazingly, nobody was hurt. The house itself was unoccupied as a newly married couple, Mr and Mrs Levene, had yet to take up residence. Despite ZA's load of aviation gasoline, prompt action by Northolt fire brigade prevented any incipient fires. A four-month-old baby in the upstairs bedroom of Number 44 was untouched and is alleged to have slept through the chaos.

But the most amazing escape of all was that of Radio Officer Hugh Murdoch. In those more casual times, he had a bad habit on take-off of standing between the pilot seats in order to look out through the windshield. Not only did he survive the crash unhurt but when he turned to look at his own seat, there was a blade of

G-AGZA resting on the roof of 46 Angus Drive, South Ruislip

the port propeller sticking through it. If he had been strapped in as regulations demanded, it is very unlikely that he would have survived.

Although Captain Johnson went on to a senior training position in BEA, he was known for the rest of his career as 'Rooftops' Johnson. Apparently the removal of ZA caused more damage than the crash itself and although repairs were completed in six months, oil stains kept re-appearing in the ceilings for the next ten years. The house was re-christened 'Dakota's Rest!'

Navigation

The lack of navigational beacons north and west of Glasgow meant that it was essential that we acquired some expertise in navigation air-plotting techniques. To this end the Pionairs had been fitted with the GEE sets which the wartime bomber fleets had used to find their targets. This system used pulses from ground-based stations displayed on early cathode ray tubes. The results could be noted on a hyperbolic chart to give a position which could then be transferred to the aircraft plotting chart. The exercise was repeated six minutes later to give an actual track and ground distance covered which could be compared to the heading and true airspeed to calculate the real wind speed and direction. If a track deviation had occurred, this new wind could be used to give the pilot an up-to-date heading to rectify the situation.

A backup was provided by the wireless direction-finding 'homers' located at the various airfields which were available on the common tower frequency of 118.3 megahertz. On the Aberdeen routes to the Orkneys and Shetland these were supplemented by Windy Head homer near Fraserburgh. Provided the aircraft was within range of two or more homers, simultaneous bearings could be requested. When these were plotted on the chart, their intersection gave a fairly accurate position and the same correction procedure was followed.

But the real role of airfield homers was to provide letdown assistance in bad weather. Only Glasgow, Aberdeen and Prestwick had the very accurate Instrument Landing System which allowed a descent to 200 feet above ground. The remaining airports had VHF Direction Finding (VDF) as their main approach aid.

In the RAF, guidance for break-cloud procedures and ground control approaches was the responsibility of skilled radar operators on the ground. As most of the peripheral civil airfields provided a flight information service rather than full air traffic control the powers-that-be had decreed that civil approaches had to be pilot-interpreted. In the resultant VDF letdown the non-handling pilot would transmit

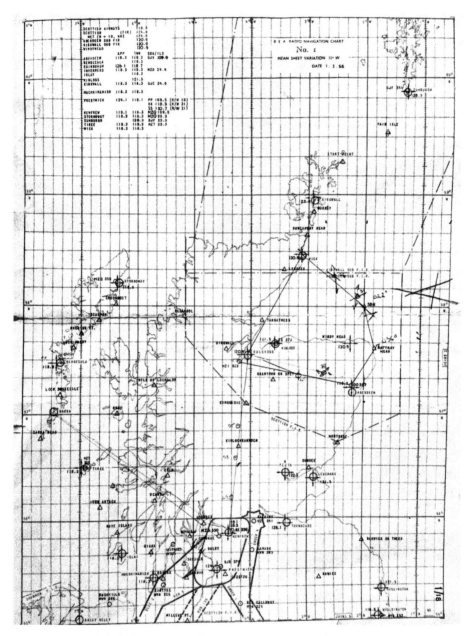

A BEA simplified plotting chart from the 50s. The route from Aberdeen to Wick had to avoid a danger area in the Moray Firth. Note that although Glasgow and Aberdeen had ILS, Edinburgh had to do without. Prestwick as an important trans-Atlantic point and diversion field had three. Inverness and Kirkwall had SBA.

for a heading to steer for the airfield. Once overhead passage was confirmed by the ground operator ('Engines overhead!') the aircraft could commence a descent outbound on a heading which would provide for a turn on to the final approach. While correcting heading towards the field was straightforward enough, the outbound tracking was another matter. In the event of deviation, clear thinking was essential in deciding which way to turn to correct the error. All this while flying on basic instruments and dealing with fickle winds, ever-varying with height.

In places like Inverness and Kirkwall, there was another relic of wartime past in the Standard Beam Approach or SBA. This installation was based on the airfield and gave an aural signal aligned with one of the runways. On the final approach you could hear the Morse letter 'A' (dot-dash) if you were left of centre line and Morse letter 'N' (dash-dot) on the right. On centre line there was a steady note. This system suffered from the same inverted-thinking difficulties as VDF when on the outbound track.

As these letdown procedures were non-precision, they were only authorised to be used down to heights of about 400 feet above the surface. Given the fickleness of the Scottish weather there were many occasions when that would not have been low enough to make sufficient visual contact to continue the approach to the runway. Old hands often used their local knowledge to apply poetic licence to the minimum descent altitude. For example, once the aeroplane passed over Benbecula heading west, there was only sea in the immediate vicinity and it was safe to cheat a little.

It was even more common to avoid the need for a letdown procedure by not entering cloud in the first place, particularly if the wind on the day required the use of a runway which had no approach guidance. The route between Stornoway and Benbecula the route was invariably flown by visual reference below cloud, down the east coast of Lewis and Harris before crossing North Uist diagonally for the airfield. It goes without saying that this required a detailed knowledge of island landmarks such as roads, houses, rocks and shorelines. Staying below the cloud base sometimes necessitated operating at some very low heights indeed. On occasion, the Dakota windscreen wipers had to be used to clear sea-spray – leaving salt deposits on the windshield by way of incriminating evidence!

Fortunately the island passengers of the time were a phlegmatic lot and seemed happy to place their trust in the pilots up front, as was demonstrated on the day my captain decided to show me the low level route between Wick and Kirkwall. The Northern Isles had an additional problem in that they were subject to that east wind coastal phenomenon of haar (or sea fog). This was the reason the SBA letdown mentioned above had been aligned on the easterly runway although the stronger prevailing winds were likely to be westerly. The rationale for our exercise was to practice for a common situation when the cloud was low and the wind was westerly. It was vital to identify the correct headland for the turn towards the runway. It was a beautiful day and we flew the whole short trip at less than a hundred feet – passing a ship in the Pentland Strait below its mast height. As we disembarked after an uneventful landing on the westerly runway, I noted with some misgiving that an elegantly dressed lady was still standing on the tarmac between us and the terminal.

'Uh oh, here comes a complaint,' I thought.

Not a bit of it.

'Captain, that was a most wonderful flight,' she smiled. 'Thank you very much!'

Even more dramatic was an occasion when I was called from standby to crew a Dakota bound for Benbecula with a replacement engine for a sick sister ship. Our only passengers were the three engineers who were going to do the engine change. Normally, the flight to Benbecula would route direct to the airport passing to the north east of the hills of my home island, South Uist. However, it was a fine spring day and, with no commercial passengers to worry about, my captain was in a relaxed mood.

Low flying over the South Uist beaches. (Painting by
Cpt. Dave Dyer in the author's collection)

Young family disembarking at Stornoway, 1960. Note the air stair door which was part of the Pionair modification.

'I think we'll go up the west coast,' he announced.

The west coast of the island is one long, silver sand beach stretching for about twenty miles and is usually deserted (although in a more benign climate it would be a mecca for sun bathers). We passed over the ferry port of Lochboisdale at about 500 feet – descending. By the time we reached the machair plain on the west side of the island, we were lower than I've ever been in a big aeroplane – before or since – and it was necessary to climb slightly to clear the sand dunes. As it happened, both my uncle and brother were on the beach that day, collecting seaweed. A few days later, a letter arrived from my brother reporting that they had seen this aeroplane coming up the beach, trailing a small whirlwind of sand behind it.

'I noted,' wrote my brother, 'that you fit Dunlop tyres to the tailwheels of Dakotas!'

I *think* he was joking.

Modern passengers, accustomed to the insulated uniformity of jets cruising high above the weather would probably be less indifferent to this occurrence than the islanders of the time. In 1982, BA celebrated the end of the Viscount era by mounting a four plane staff expedition to Orkney. The pilots exuberantly re-visited some of the customs of old by skimming across the Pentland Strait at heights well below the Orkney cliffs. Despite the fact that the passengers all had a close connection with the airline, it was noticeable that a slight unease had dulled the party atmosphere.

Characters

Eventually my training captains were persuaded that I had learnt enough to be released to the line as a fully functioning second pilot. They made clear, however, that they had only provided me with a dummy's survival guide. There was still much to learn from the captains I would fly with. Initially, these would be the more experienced hands for whom Glasgow was their preferred home base rather than those new commands who regarded it as a rude but temporary interruption of their London career. Some of the older generation were less than delighted at

The flight clerk assists in unloading newspapers from the Pionair's forward hold. © Ralph Landells

changes such as the newfangled reliance on drill cards and regarded the monitored approach with some suspicion. But generally the *esprit de corps* at Renfrew was high and there was a friendliness and mutual respect pervading the entire station which was still small enough for all grades of staff to be on first name terms and consider themselves part of the same team.

In particular, flying was shared most of the time on a fifty-fifty basis between captain and co-pilot. This was very important for the latter as hours had to be built up for those more senior licences essential for promotion. The non-handling pilot was responsible for navigation, radio and, in the absence of cabin address, drafting a bulletin on progress to be passed back to the passengers. This could usually be filled out in advance with just arrival time to be confirmed.

One trip to Inverness taught me a small lesson in passenger psychology. I had recorded our projected cruising level as the usual 7,500 feet but on this occasion we were restricted to 5,500. Shortly after this misleading bulletin was passed back, the flight clerk reported that an elderly lady was having difficulty breathing at 7,500 feet. We suggested he should tell her we would descend to 5,500. He returned a few minutes later with the news that she was now feeling much better.

Although there was much to learn even as co-pilot, it was the hours operating as the handling pilot – or P1 under supervision as it was called – which were really important. These counted in full for the minima required when improving our basic Commercial Pilot licences through Senior Commercial Pilot to the ultimate Airline Transport Pilot Licence (ATPL) necessary to operate in command. Even though that felt but a distant dream, I was still studying hard for the obligatory theoretical exams.

From a handling point of view, the Scottish weather ensured that the learning curve was steep. One slight drawback to gaining experience was that eventually you were deemed competent enough to fly with the new captains, of which Glasgow (as the junior base) had a constant turnover. New commands were not allowed to give landings to co-pilots till they had accumulated at least 100 hours in the left-hand seat themselves. At the height of the training season this could be a frustrating time for second officers desperate to build up their hours and landings. However, most new captains were charming and pleasant guys just as eager to learn as we were so the operation was still fun.

For all its camaraderie, the Glasgow base did have one significant drawback for those of us so recently released from the monastic lifestyle of the RAF. Our dreams of glamorous hostesses suffered a cruel blow when we discovered that on Scottish services the Dakota cabin was supervised by a single male flight clerk. Apart from keeping an eye on the passengers, their muscle power was required in turnarounds to help in the loading and unloading of baggage, mail and newspapers at stations with minimum staff.

There was no passenger meal catering equipment on the Scottish internal services so the refreshment provided to sustain the crew through some long duty days was a cardboard box with ham and cheese sandwiches and an iconic Scottish chocolate biscuit. Passenger catering was provided on services such as Glasgow–London and included red and white wine. The red was dry and fairly acrid while the white was rather sweet. By process of experiment it was soon discovered that a judicious blending of the two could provide a reasonably palatable rose.

To be fair to our flight clerks, most of them were interesting characters in their own right and there was some compensation in that the Renfrew traffic staff included some very attractive young ladies. In fact there seemed to be as many characters among the ground staff as there were among the pilots, particularly at the much smaller out-stations.

At Benbecula, the station was run by Donald MacDonald with the help of Margaret Macpherson. Donald had been with Scottish Aviation in the days when Benbecula was still a grass field. This explained why part of his earlier job description had required him to have a dog – to clear the sheep off the aerodrome before the plane's arrival. Given that the start-up of Dakota Pratt & Whitney engines was sometimes accompanied by bursts of flame, his duties now included standing by with fire extinguisher at the ready.

The station at Tiree was run by the tall, gangling figure of Colin Macphail with Mary Munn as assistant. Colin had been a shepherd before he was engaged by Northern and Scottish Airways in 1936 to supervise aircraft arrivals on the machair at Reef. In a fine example of multi-tasking he was also a lay preacher and special constable while running his own croft. It was not unknown for him to turn up to meet the aeroplane in wellington boots liberally spattered with evidence that he had been cleaning out the byres.

Station Superintendent Benbecula Donald MacDonald with the fire extinguisher used to monitor engine start-up.

Colin's manner was a fine example of that Highland courtesy that treats all with respect without undue deference to any. The most famous example was reported in a story BEA's chairman, Lord Douglas of Kirtleside, told of an occasion when he was making a ceremonial round of the Scottish stations. Accustomed to the flurry of excitement his arrival would normally generate, he was somewhat underwhelmed by his reception at Tiree. Eventually he met Colin.

'Weren't you expecting me?' he enquired.

'If you're Lord Douglas of Kirtleside, I am,' came the reply which has gone down in history. 'If you're not, I'm not!'

At Campbeltown, the station superintendent, Jimmy McGeachy, also ran the town hardware shop where he had a special counter dedicated to the sale of airline tickets. When customers arrived in search of such, he would transfer in a dignified manner to the BEA counter and don his official cap before embarking on the transaction.

The men who provided the Air Information Service at the various airports were also individual characters. In the days before all air traffic transmissions were recorded, they often featured a considerable amount of banter. As the Dakota taxied in at Wick one day, the incumbent in the tower locked down his transmit key and played a brisk *Rule Britannia* on his penny whistle. He then came on air and made a solemn request for a sound check.

'Bealine Yankee Fox, do you detect a loud background whistle to my transmissions?'

Another anecdote records the experience of a man alleged to be BEA's most satisfied customer. At the time there was an air link between Edinburgh and Glasgow, designed to offer citizens of the capital a connecting service to Glasgow's more extensive network. In the 50s the return fare was a mere £1, which was noted by a canny Edinburgher as being by far the cheapest way of gaining his first experience of flight. Thus one fine winter's morning found him in the Edinburgh terminal in happy anticipation of an exciting new experience. Unfortunately, as so often happened in coal fire days, Glasgow had smog problems. BEA apologised several times for a delay to the service and eventually announced that passengers could repair to the restaurant for lunch.

After lunch came the usual improvement in visibility and the passengers were led out to the aircraft which eventually roared off into the ether. Seated at his window our man revelled in wonderful views of the Forth Rail Bridge, distant mountains of the Highlands and even Loch Lomond as the Pionair started describing lazy circles in the sky over Glasgow. As so often happened, the smog

Pionair on 10-minute turn round at Benbecula. Only the left engine was shut down.

had thickened again and with further apology the aeroplane diverted back to Edinburgh. Passengers were given the option of being taken to the railway station or having their money back.

'I'll have my money back, thanks very much!'

John Welford

One man more than any other generated legendary anecdotes that have become permanently woven into the fabric of aviation folklore: Captain John W. Welford (known as Jack to his friends and John Willie to co-pilots outwith his hearing). In his mature years he bore a passing resemblance to bearded character actor James Robertson Justice and he displayed a level of eccentricity even more extreme than the latter's on- and off-screen persona.

The BEA staff magazine features Captain JW Welford in 1949.

Welford's most notorious prank featured early in his career when he was still on the Rapide. He would board in a civilian coat and take one of the passenger seats. As time of departure approached, there would start a crescendo of grumbling about the punctuality of the airline.

'Do you know, if this damn pilot doesn't turn up soon, I might fly the thing myself!'

The rest of the passengers, being a stoical lot, would ignore these ravings until they culminated in:

'That does it!'

And he would stomp up to the single pilot cockpit and start up.

There is evidence that this trick was repeated several times and undoubtedly the tale has been embroidered over the years. Some versions have JW boarding in dark glasses with a white stick; others have the aeroplane roaring down the runway while Welford boomed to the Radio Officer,

'Is this the thing you pull back on to get off the ground?'

Variations of this story have passed into world aviation folklore and, as is the nature of these things, have not only been embellished but also attributed to other pilots known to the narrator – including, apparently, myself.

Less well known is the episode which brought the curtain down on this particular part of the Welford repertoire. On one occasion he had on board a large and sturdy Scot who took no notice of his fellow passenger's ramblings until the lunatic entered the cockpit and started the engines. The islander then took the view that, whatever the possible outcome might be, he wanted no part of it and decided to get off. In his attempts to abandon ship the aircraft door was so damaged that the flight was brought to a premature conclusion.

Although BEA completely failed to see the joke, the irrepressible Welford soon found other outlets for his sense of humour. Boarding the Dakota one day after the passengers, he got as far as the open cockpit door before turning to favour them with a dazzling smile. He then closed the door behind him to reveal the L plate hanging behind it.

The Dakota had one solitary toilet (Elsan-equipped) in the rear of the cabin. As his aeroplane cruised through the skies one day, he emerged from the cockpit backwards, unrolling two balls of string before stopping by the side of a middle aged lady, quietly minding her own business.

'Would you mind helping me out, madam?' he enquired, handing her the two balls of string.

'Just got to nip to the loo,' he continued. 'If the left wing drops, pull on the right string and if the right wing drops, pull on the left!'

Before she had time to react, he was off, leaving the terrified woman clutching the strings – while the co-pilot had been instructed to keep her busy by weaving gently through the sky.

In 1958, Welford was based in Aberdeen where BEA maintained a small group of three captains and three co-pilots to operate the Orkney and Shetland services out of Dyce. Leave and sickness requirements necessitated that relief pilots had to be posted in from the larger Glasgow base. Having heard all the tales of eccentricity, it was with some alarm that, in August 1958, I discovered that I was to be sent to Aberdeen for a fortnight to act as Welford's co-pilot.

BEA's night stop hotel, the Caledonian in Union Terrace, was to be my home for that period. Nowadays posh hotels have discovered a money-spinner in that they can demand more for afternoon tea than many restaurants charge for dinner. It is interesting to reflect that in the late 50s the Caley's rate was two shillings and sixpence (12½p). For that modest outlay a waitress would bring a handsome pot of tea and the standard three-tiered cake stand. The bottom layer held a selection of sandwiches; the middle was devoted to scones with butter and jam; the top was crowned with a delicious selection of cakes. It is fair to say that, even then, this must have been a loss leader geared to the middle class Aberdeen housewife in shopping mode who might toy with the odd cake or two. Impecunious young BEA second officers, however, would devour the lot and might not need to have dinner!

Breakfast was even more impressive. After the usual orange juice and porridge, the Caledonian mixed grill included all the standard features plus a lamb chop. With the healthy appetite of youth, I had polished this lot off one morning when the elderly waiter shuffled over. Without a hint of irony in the voice he produced a classic example of dry Aberdonian wit,

'Anything else, sir ... a pair of kippers maybe?'

It must be remembered that in those days even one Aberdeen kipper was a fine sight to behold compared to today's scrawny offerings. I was compelled to decline his kind offer.

*Sumburgh, Shetland in 1958. Thanks to the oil business
it is nowadays one of the busiest airports in Scotland.*

The much smaller Aberdeen terminal of the 50s was located on the opposite side of the main runway from the current edifice and it was there that I reported for my very first meeting with Captain Welford for a flight to Sumburgh in Shetland. This was not only one of the longest sectors in the Scottish network but also, being largely over water and out of sight of land, required some careful navigation plotting by the non-handling pilot. Busily getting and plotting bearings from Wick, Windy Head and Aberdeen homers (all on the common frequency of 118.3), I was startled when my Captain broke a few minutes silence with the mysterious transmission, 'Knight to Queen Five!' I looked around in wild surmise, fearing I was trapped in the middle of nowhere with a captain who had finally lost his marbles. However, everything continued normally. The following day we were in approximately the same position when an anonymous voice spoke out of the ether and said, 'Pawn to King Six!'. Welford was conducting a one-move-a-day chess game with one of the controllers on the common frequency. My other memory of that fortnight reminds us how quiet the Scottish aviation scene of the 50s was. On a long turnaround at Turnhouse (Edinburgh) my captain wandered off across the middle of the airport on a mushroom hunt. Of course, Edinburgh today is the busiest airport in Scotland

When the time came for my return to Glasgow he graciously signed my logbook confirming the landings I had been given and filled in a confidential report to the effect that I might make a good first officer – in time!

Christmas Eve that year saw Scotland blanketed in fog and the futuristic little Renfrew terminal chock-a-block with passengers desperate to get home for Christmas. Welford also was unable to depart for Aberdeen and at one point I watched him commandeer the PA system to entertain the assembled punters with Christmas carols.

My colleague Geoff Northmore was for a time based at Aberdeen and therefore had more exposure to the Welford brand of eccentricity. He recalled the departure of the London flight being announced while they were having a cup of tea in the terminal. Welford suddenly snatched up a potted plant from an adjacent table and strode out to the line of boarding passengers. Seizing on a respectable looking city gent, he boomed,

'Congratulations, sir, you are the ten thousandth passenger on this service this year; please accept a small token of our esteem,' before presenting the somewhat bemused passenger with a fine example of the airport's best household plants!

Geoff also remembered that Welford grew tired of a particular passenger at Wick who always arrived at the very last minute, thereby causing delay to a ten minute turnaround. One day he waited till the repeat offender had his first foot on the air stair door before releasing the brakes. As the Dakota moved slowly off, the passenger hopped along with it, presumably learning his lesson.

His concern for passengers was perhaps better demonstrated on another occasion at Wick when the flight was delayed. Welford assembled his passengers in military style inside the hangar and roared out the order 'Follow me!' before marching them off to lunch at a nearby restaurant.

However amusing some of these anecdotes may be in this age of standard operating procedures and inflexible bureaucracy, it may be of some comfort to nervous passengers to know that his type of larger-than-life eccentricity would have little chance of surviving modern airline selection procedures.

The Heron and Air Ambulance

*H*ad the aviation accident rate of the 50s continued to the present day, we would be witnessing a jumbo crash every week. Amazingly, the record of BEA' s passenger service in Scotland was excellent, despite

Heron G-ANXB on ambulance duty at Barra 1959. Note the sister from the Southern General Hospital in front of the terminal building.

THIS CAIRN ALSO
PAYS HOMAGE TO THE
MEMORY OF THE FOLLOWING
MEMBERS OF THE SERVICE WHO
LOST THEIR LIVES AT ISLAY
WHEN ANSWERING A CALL FOR
HELP ON 28TH SEPTEMBER, 1957

CAPTAIN T. M. CALDERWOOD
RADIO OFFICER H. McGINLAY
NURSING SISTER J. KENNEDY

The names of those
who in their lives fought for life.
Who wore at their hearts
the fires centre.
Born of the sun, they travelled
a short while towards the sun
And left the vivid air
signed with their honour.

*Heron memorial near the
site of Renfrew airport.*

the lack of navigation aids and appalling winter weather which often tempted pilots to make some very liberal interpretations of the prescribed descent limits. It is a remarkable tribute to the training and personal skill of so many individuals.

Uniquely, in BEA the ambulance service was given carte-blanche to operate in any weather at the captain's discretion. Personal experience and local knowledge did much to compensate for lack of navigational and descent aids. In 1955 the trusty Rapides had been replaced by three much more modern deHavilland Herons. Four engines gave the ability to carry double the Rapide passenger load and made for much better all-weather aircraft. Given de Havilland's reputation for building sweet-handling aeroplanes, the Heron was a much more comfortable ambulance capable of carrying two stretchers if need be.

However, in 1957 disaster struck. On a filthy night on 28 September, Captain Paddy Calderwood was called out with Radio Officer Hugh McGinlay for an ambulance case in Islay. The nurse on board (as usual from the Southern General Hospital) was Sister Jean Kennedy. The wind direction was such that a landing could not be made direct from the approach procedure. In the subsequent low level circuit in the dark, the Heron struck the ground and all three were killed.

When the news got back to Glasgow, Flight Manager Eric Starling volunteered to take a replacement Heron to resume the mercy mission. It is said that when the nurses at the Southern General were asked if any would be prepared to go, all the qualified sisters volunteered. Sadly, their brave efforts were in vain for the patient died.

One of the consequences was to have an important impact on the lives of Glasgow's co-pilots. Great improvements in the radio-telephone network had removed the need for a specialised Morse code qualified radio officer. Although the Heron was cleared for single pilot operation it was decided that it would be much safer to have a second pilot, better able to monitor and assist the captain in difficult situations.

Captain Ralph Landells' son John tries out the co-pilot's seat in Heron 1b G-ANXA. Note the absence of flight instruments in the panel in front of him. © Ralph Landells

The good news for us Dakota co-pilots would be that we could also fly on the Heron and experience the job satisfaction of ambulance work. The bad news was that we would not be given the training to have the aircraft on our licences and, therefore, the flying time would not count towards those precious senior licence requirements. In practice, the lack of technical qualification troubled our captains not at all. They quite happily shared the flying with us in the usual way. There was a slight handicap in bad weather in that the only instrument panel was on the captain's side but we quickly adjusted to flying in cloud by looking to our left. It helped that the Heron was such an easy and delightful aeroplane to handle.

There were two outstanding bonuses. Firstly, we could now fly with two living legends in the contrasting shapes of Captain David Barclay (who was short) and Captain Eric Starling (who was tall). Secondly, the Heron's bread and butter passenger route was the Tiree–Barra service which involved landing on Barra's iconic beach. That was why BEA had preferred the Heron 1b version with fixed undercarriage to the Mark 2 with its retractable underpinnings. The effect of salt water on aluminium makes it a very poor idea to retract wheels which have been exposed to brine into the complex and delicate innards of an aircraft wing. It was essential to wash the aircraft down each time it returned from a beach landing.

It was in August of 1958 that I first flew with David Barclay to the beach where he had inaugurated the air service to Barra in 1936. Although David had been Scottish Airways chief pilot, one would have never guessed from this little man's unassuming air that he had done so much to pioneer air routes and landing places throughout the islands. As mentioned earlier, he now flew only on the Heron because his wartime accident had deprived one leg of the strength to cope with a low-speed engine failure on the Dakota. Many have had cause to be grateful that by the time of his eventual retirement in 1965 this legendary pioneer had completed over 1,200 ambulance flights.

David was one of the old school of pilots who were accustomed to relying on their instinctive feel for an aeroplane and comprehensive knowledge of weather and terrain gained from long experience. This could sometimes be alarming for his new co-pilots, who were more accustomed to relying on newfangled instrument approaches.

Katie Macpherson and Captain David Barclay, Barra 1958.

Captain David Barclay © Bruce Cousins

My old colleague Arthur Downes embarked on his first trip with David on one of those soggy Hebridean days when the cloud base at Barra seemed to hold out little chance of a successful arrival. Barra at the time had no letdown aids of any description. True, the Heron did have an early Decca Navigator system where signals from three transmitters could be received on dials and plotted by the co-pilot on a map showing the transmission patterns. This was useful insofar as finding Barra was concerned but of limited value as a letdown aid. The standard practice, therefore, was to stay below cloud on departing from Tiree and skim the waves until landmarks could be identified. Arthur was busy getting used to his new duties and didn't take too much notice when David asked for the landing checks.

'Suddenly,' he said, 'this lunatic closed the throttles and landed in the sea!'

Fortunately, the 'sea' was only an inch deep at this point and the Heron trundled safely across the beach.

'How did you know where we were?' asked Arthur.

'We passed that buoy which marks the entrance to the bay!' explained David.

'What if it had drifted loose?' pondered Arthur silently.

In better weather it was customary to overfly the beach first to check the surface and state of the tide before landing. Famously, the Barra timetable was annotated

'Times subject to tides' but although the times of low tides can be predicted with considerable accuracy that was no guarantee of the state of the beach. An onshore easterly gale could hold the water onsite longer whereas a westerly could help clear the water faster. Traditional wisdom held that if the seagulls were standing it was safe to land; if they were swimming it was not.

My own first arrival at Barra was, as usual, greeted by Katie Macpherson, the lovely lady who ran Barra airport for thirty years. For much of that time she was effectively a one-woman band with the assistance of Donald Sinclair who drove the fire engine and helped with the baggage. Katie was the daughter of John Macpherson, nicknamed the Coddy, who had suggested to David Barclay in 1935 that the beach might be a suitable landing place. The Coddy became the little airport's first station superintendent.

Island shops of the 50s were limited both by the range of available goods and the erratic supply from the mainland by ferry three times a week. As the most regular operator to Tiree and Barra, David was happy to pick up fresh groceries for the station staff on his way into work. On one famous occasion he checked into the Operations room at Renfrew to be told:

'There's no load into or out of Tiree today, David, so it's just Barra and back.'

'But,' expostulated David, 'I've got the messages [shopping] for Tiree!'

'Definitely no need to land in Tiree today.'

As it happened, Scottish Air Traffic Control had just begun to record all transmissions on their frequencies; a practice which is universal nowadays. A few weeks later a sheet of paper appeared on the notice board in the crew room. It was a transcript from the Scottish Air Traffic Control frequency covering Tiree and it provoked much crew hilarity.

'Tiree, this is Bealine XB, we won't be landing today but I've got the messages. I'll just fly past the tower and drop them off for you!'

'Tiree, XB, just running from the South, here go the sausages! Will be back with the bread in a minute!'

A shower of small packages descended from the open side window of a very low-flying Heron before it came round for a second pass.

'There's the bread!'

The views of the passengers on this vital supplies drop were not recorded but David had accrued enough seniority in Scotland to be a law unto himself.

Barra was not the only destination which required a beach landing. Before 1960, there was no causeway connection between Benbecula and North Uist. Although the latter had actually had its own grass airfield prior to the war, plans for a great military expansion had been abandoned in the Duncan Sandys cutbacks of 1957. As a result, the wide sandy beaches at Sollas had to be pressed into service for any ambulance flights. In bad weather the Committee road across the island became a convenient guide to the landing area.

The doctors at Lochmaddy were a husband and wife team, Alex and Julia Macleod. As well as concern for their patients, their solicitude extended to the ambulance crew and they would greet the aircraft armed with a basket of delicious sandwiches and a flask of coffee. Given the absence of any catering facility on the Heron, the subsequent picnic on the machair while the patient was loaded on board was a very welcome interlude. Their son John eventually succeeded them in the Lochmaddy practice and was happy to show me the original basket and flask some thirty years later.

The late Dr John Macleod of North Uist with the basket and flask that his parents used in providing alfresco lunches for air ambulance pilots landing on the beach at Sollas.

There is no doubt that many lives were saved thanks to the Heron's sterling service. However, its take-off and landing distance requirements rendered it unsuitable for the smaller islands. In February 1957 an attempt had been made to include Coll in its repertoire but the collapse of an undercarriage leg on landing suggested this was not a good idea. In 1962 the Scottish airline Loganair made a modest start with a couple of small Piper aircraft. But when they acquired the Britten Norman Islander in 1967 they were able to utilise that aircraft's brilliant short field performance to expand the air ambulance service to Colonsay, Mull, Oronsay and Oban as well as Coll.

As their passenger network expanded to include the Orkneys and Shetland, so the ambulance service broadened out to many islands hitherto difficult of access. In 1973, Loganair was awarded the full air ambulance contract for Scotland. At various times this service was complemented by the added flexibility of helicopters from the RAF, Navy and Coastguard.

Loganair Britten Norman Islander at Broadford, Skye 1974.

Islander with ambulance Barra © Cpt. Dave Dyer

Not least of the air ambulance duties was ferrying expectant mothers to the better facilities of mainland hospitals. Sometimes the call-out cut things a little too fine. My friend Captain David Dyer at one time claimed the Loganair record for the number of babies born on his flights – at four. One of them was a boy for Mrs Margaret Ayres from Islay. As they routed into Glasgow David asked the happy mother whether she would like her son's birth registered in Gourock or Kilmacolm. The family were so grateful to the air ambulance service that they decided to christen their new arrival Jonathan Logan Ayres!

Nowadays, the air ambulance service is a fully funded part of NHS Scotland. In 2018 it operated two King Air 200c twin turboprop aircraft for conventional airports with two Airbus H145 helicopters for more challenging call-outs.

The Viscount

Few people today will remember how much the Vickers Viscount revolutionised 50s air travel for the passenger. Driven by four Rolls Royce Dart turboprops, it was twice as fast as the Dakota, carried twice as many passengers and its pressurised hull enabled it to operate at over 20,000 feet – above much of the bad weather and associated turbulence. The smoothly spinning Dart turbines provided a huge advance in passenger comfort compared to the noise and vibration of reciprocating piston engines. Adverts showed passengers balancing the old three penny bits on edge to demonstrate the difference. Huge windows gave excellent views.

Viscount 700 at Renfrew in 1959.

Passengers boarding a Viscount 806 for London Airport at Renfrew, 1959.

For their European services, BEA bought Viscount 700 series crewed by two pilots and a radio officer. We had occasionally operated our Pionairs to London Airport (as Heathrow was known at the time) but more and more of these services were taken over by the Viscount which halved the schedule time to one hour and twenty five minutes. Given the congested skies and consequent delays of today, even the modern jet sometimes has difficulty in matching Viscount times on short sectors. At the time, the schedules posed new challenges for the cabin crew as the prestige evening routes had full 'Silver Wing' meal service in first class.

For another member of the crew the writing was on the wall. With improvements in plain speech radio telephone communication throughout the civilised world, the era of the specialised radio officer with his Morse key was coming to an end. Vickers produced an even more advanced version – the Viscount 800 series – with the operating crew reduced to two pilots. As some compensation for the unfortunate radio officers, pilot conversion courses were offered to those who preferred them to redundancy payments.

Various models of the Viscount 800 became the standard workhorse for short haul airlines around the world – even penetrating the American market. It is still the best-selling British commercial airliner of all time. BEA had two versions: the 802 and the more powerful 806 which operated in a two class configuration. Two-man operation of an aeroplane capable of 300 mph in the busy European air lanes was considered such a challenge that pilot union BALPA managed to negotiate a handsome pay increase on the back of the improved productivity.

This made it even more of an object of desire for humble Dakota pilots. There was considerable excitement in the Renfrew crew room when we heard of the imminent arrival of the first 806. Out we rushed to watch the shiny silver machine come whistling over the threshold of runway 26. It struck the ground a mighty blow and bounced before arriving at a second attempt nose wheel first. We gazed at each other in awed surmise. Clearly only supermen could cope with this advanced machine! Fortunately we were later to discover that the Viscount was actually one of the nicest landing aeroplanes a pilot could hope to meet. The snag at the time was that most of them were based in London.

With the passing of exams for the senior licences came promotion from second officer to first officer. The consequent boost in income allowed me to graduate from a little Austin A35 to a second-hand MG Magnette ZB saloon in damask red. With its leather upholstery and polished wooden dashboard it seemed to me to be the very epitome of a British gentleman's sporting carriage! Thanks to a 95% mortgage from the Abbey National I had just bought my first flat in Pollokshields on the south side of Glasgow as well. For the very reasonable sum of £1,000 I was now the proud owner of a Victorian tenement residence which, in estate agent jargon, boasted two massive reception rooms, three bedrooms, a butler's pantry and maid's room. The bargain price was due to the fact that these Victorian flats had a high rateable value. As they were also free from any vestige of central heating, their cavernous rooms cost a fortune to heat. Coal fires were labour intensive and electric bars fought a losing battle against the Glasgow winters. A new BEA recruit, Bruce Cousins, was persuaded to share some of the expense, although he was forever disappearing off on twelve-hour journeys to London in his Morris Minor to see his girlfriend Ailsa. We were to become life-long friends.

In addition to my commercial flying I had also renewed my love affair with the Chipmunk through joining the RAFVR Air Experience Flight at Edinburgh Turnhouse. As the name implies, this unit existed in order to offer Air Training Corps and Combined Cadet Force teenagers the opportunity of a twenty-minute flight in a trainer aircraft. The cadets varied in their reactions from the wildly enthusiastic to the slightly terrified but it was amazing what one could achieve with one of the former in just twenty minutes. It was a point of honour with me not to do aerobatics unless the cadet actually sounded positive about the idea but the usage of sick bags suggested that perhaps some of my colleagues were less understanding!

With my new-found expertise on crosswind landings, I did try to influence RAF thinking away from the 'kick-off-drift' mentality which had so traumatised my own early efforts. But, although Dakota technique worked equally well on Chipmunks, suggestions from my lowly level fell on stony ground.

All in all, I was very happy at the small but friendly Renfrew base. The routes became familiar although the weather could be the most challenging in the airline's network. The restricted facilities of outlying Scottish airports placed a huge premium on the honing of basic skills but, by and large, the lack of much in the way of airport lighting made for a lifestyle mostly confined to daylight hours. This meant that I could indulge a passion for amateur drama. In Scotland in the days before TV really took hold, many amateur clubs had high production values and could command large audiences.

From a career point of view, however, promotion to more modern and exciting aeroplanes was only possible at London. So, with some misgiving, the youthful desire for newer toys urged me to apply for Viscount 800s. Years later I was to muse occasionally on what might have happened had I remained in Scotland. I had already taken part in the odd radio broadcast and when TV eventually flourished in Glasgow, many of those in the amateur drama scene became heavily involved in the early years. Tempting though it might be to think that one 'might have been a contender', experience of the TV world much later in life confirmed that my decision had been the correct one.

On Saturday, 19 November 1960, I played the part of the heartless villain in the Torch Club performance of Victorian melodrama *East Lynne*. It was a full house at the old Empress theatre by St George's Cross. Twenty four hours later I embarked with the Magnette overnight on the pre-motorway 12-hour slog to London.

London Airport

With the resilience of youth I was able to catch up on some sleep on the Monday before next morning renewing my acquaintance with Viking Centre, BEA's training unit under the approach path to London Airport's southerly runway, 28 Left. There

Viscount 806 © BA

we grappled with the mysteries of electrical and hydraulic systems considerably more sophisticated than those of the Pionair.

In particular, the cockpit was a brave new world. BEA had ventured into hitherto untraveled territory for Britain by attempting to apply the science of ergonomics to its design. Instead of being randomly sprinkled round various panels as of yore, the numerous supplementary switches and dials had been grouped in accordance with function. The new Smiths System SEP 2 autopilot had been integrated with the flight instruments. As well as simpler tasks such as holding heading or altitude it was capable of useful tricks such as locking on to a VOR radial en-route or an ILS approach to the runway.

The ground course culminated on 30 December with the Air Registration Board's technical exam. Set by engineers, these tests were universally loathed by pilots for an emphasis on technical bits of kit which we had no way of accessing in flight. The pass mark was something like 85% but, thanks to some friendly tips on possible questions, we all passed.

Three days later on 2 January 1961, the next stage introduced us to a training device which was to become a major feature of our future careers – the simulator. There had been nothing so modern available for the Dakota so all training and checks had been conducted on the aeroplane. This early example for the Viscount 800 was a fairly convincing replica of the cockpit in which all the ground and flight procedures could be practised. Not only did the instruments work and respond to the controls and switches but by dint of a camera travelling over a map outside we had a hazy view of terrain through the windows. It was a crude and earthbound device compared to modern simulators, which generate a better feeling of realistic motion through being mounted on hydraulic jacks. Even then, however, it was considered good enough to be used for six-monthly competency checks and the annual essential Instrument Rating Tests of our ability to operate in cloud.

At long last, on 8 January, came the moment every converting pilot eagerly anticipated. Base training gives the chance to fly the real aeroplane without having to worry about the effect of any initial bumbling on passenger morale. With Captain Dougie Lee we took off from London Airport in Viscount 802 G-AOJD and climbed up high to explore our new toy's handling in steep turns and stalls before arriving at Stansted airport. In those days of the 60s it had so little traffic that it was a convenient place for pilots to practise take-offs and landings.

Over the next three days we discovered that the Viscount was indeed a civilised aeroplane to fly and rewarding to land. In traditional aircrew fashion, evenings in the pub were passed in comparing notes, exchanging stories and extracting any bit of useful information we could from our more experienced trainers. Having demonstrated we could cope with engine failures on take-off, three-engine overshoots and landings we were eventually signed off for the final stage of training – on the line with real passengers.

After a quick visit to Glasgow, six days later I reported to the Queen's Building at London Airport at half past six on the morning of 16 January. The future site of Terminal 1 was just a green field which served as a crew car park. Day one of my roster had three short flights: a return jaunt to Manchester followed by a Paris night stop. Fortunately, my training captain was Tom Griffiths who was an absolute gentleman determined to pass on to me as much as he could of his own expertise.

The much-anticipated night stop was my first visit to Paris and I revelled in the new experience. Concern had been rising about levels of liver disease in France and posters in the Metro helpfully pointed out that it was injurious to health to drink more than two litres of wine a day!

After a splendid meal in a local bistro we found a little theatre where an assortment of very attractive ladies seemed delighted to take all their clothes off on stage. Revelatory although this was to one who had hitherto led a sheltered life, it would undoubtedly be considered demure by the internet-hardened teenagers of today. Sadly, there are relatively few variations on the basic stripping formula, so by the end of the evening a certain level of ennui had set in.

In the early 60s BEA used Le Bourget for Paris flights. In those more leisurely days, the lunchtime schedule actually allowed the crew enough time to have a sit-down meal. The airport restaurant was usually ignored in favour of crossing the road to a little place which complied with two basic requirements of a French bistro:

a) The menu should be chalk-written on a blackboard.

b) It should be full of French people.

Although BEA stood for British European Airways, its route network was by no means as constricted as the name implies. Before Cyprus

Viscount 806 cabin crew at Le Bourget, Paris, 1960.

BEA Viscount 806 G-AOYN at a deserted Benghazi in November, 1962.

and Malta had their own airline fleets, BEA provided the necessary services. Within a couple of weeks of Tom signing me off as a competent co-pilot I was in Nicosia again on the way to Beirut across the desert to Kuwait and then down the Persian Gulf. We routed via Bahrain to night stop at Doha – then just a quiet little town.

The lack of radio aids in the area was brought home to us on the return journey. Between Kuwait and Beirut it became obvious that headwinds were much stronger than forecast. Although an oil pipeline was of useful navigational assistance in so far as our track was concerned, there were few opportunities for a groundspeed check. For a time there was some doubt as to whether we had enough fuel to make Beirut.

For Malta Airlines we operated into Tripoli and Benghazi in North Africa. Pre-Ghadaffi Libya produced vast quantities of cheap wine; much of it, we understood, bound for France where it was likely to end up in bottles labelled Bordeaux. North Africa was deemed somewhat exotic by BEA, so when we night-stopped in Tripoli we were entitled to an individual bottle of mineral water with dinner. The Italian mineral water was actually more expensive than the local wine so the waiter taking orders would ask, 'And the Pellegrino – red or white?' It is shameful to report that the incidence of those taking the implied option led to some very quiet taxi rides back to the airport in the morning.

Operating into Benghazi, we were often the only aeroplane on the tarmac, save perhaps for a transiting military charter. Our hotel in town was conspicuously less grand than the one in Tripoli. The Viscount had only two cabin crew, usually one male and one female. BEA had booked two sets of adjoining rooms which shared a bathroom. Invariably the co-pilot found himself next door to the steward while the receptionist, with an evil glint in his eye, allocated the stewardess a room next to the captain.

The hopes of my generation that the tide would turn in our favour once we had reached the dizzy heights of command were to be cruelly dashed. As colleague Ken Beere pointed out, round about the age of 28, the permissive society of the 60s passed us going in the other direction. It was now the young cadets fresh from the college at Hamble who were the centre of female attention.

The other service we operated out of Malta was a thirty-five-minute hop across the Mediterranean to Catania in Sicily. The infrequency of our visits to the airport did not warrant the presence of a BEA ground engineer so we carried one with us from Malta. As we taxied out at Luqa one fine August afternoon, my captain suddenly grimaced. When I enquired as to the problem, he mentioned a stabbing pain but said he was OK again. However, during the short flight it became obvious that he was in trouble. On the ground at Catania we had a discussion. It was clear he was now in severe pain and in need of medical help. However, none of us had much knowledge of the standard of Sicilian hospitals of the time whereas we knew Malta had excellent facilities. A further consideration was that a full load of passengers was waiting for the flight. It was decided that I would fly the aeroplane back with the engineer acting as an unofficial monitoring crew member. I gave him the checklist and asked him to ensure that nothing was missed. Our ailing captain was the ultimate back-up.

Back we flew without any further drama except for my request to Luqa tower that an ambulance should meet the aircraft. Naturally no mention was made of the fact that it was the captain who had the problem. He was safely transferred to Malta's premier hospital where it transpired he had a kidney stone, generally reckoned to be the male equivalent of childbirth. It was my first and only flight in command of a Viscount. But those were different times. Impossible to imagine a similar decision being taken in today's bureaucratic environment.

The other major area of operation for the Viscount had come about because of the Cold War. After the partitioning of Germany, West Berlin had become a little oasis of freedom within the eastern Soviet-controlled German Democratic Republic. Three narrow air corridors connected the pre-war Berlin airport of Templehof with the western Federal Republic of Germany. Famously, these three lanes had managed to keep the city supplied via the Berlin Airlift when the Russians had blocked surface routes in 1948. In 1949 the Soviets eventually conceded that they could not isolate the city and commercial services gradually developed. However, they were only allowed to be operated by the occupying powers of the United States, Britain and France. By the 60s the bulk of flights were provided by Pan Am and BEA with a few by Air France.

The Soviets made it as difficult as possible for the western airlines. There was an ever-present threat that any aircraft straying outside the corridors might be intercepted by fighters and no flights were permitted above 10,000 feet. This not only made for uneconomical operation for modern aircraft but also presented problems for passenger comfort and aircraft safety in summer when thunderclouds were common. For these reasons, captains had to be specially cleared for the Berlin operation and flights were closely monitored by American military radar. The emphasis on route experience tended to restrict the operation to a proportion of available captains.

Despite potential operational problems, generous meal allowances made tours to Germany very popular with many pilots. In those heady days when the pound was still a major currency, it could be exchanged for about twelve marks. That made the bustling city of West Berlin with its busy night life a very cheap place to have a good time. For those of a cultural bent, seats could be had to enjoy the Deutsch Opera's parade of stars for the equivalent of six pounds.

A special flight of German-speaking stewardesses was established at Templehof. As some captains spent most of their working life on the German Internals (as they were known), it is not surprising that some liaisons led to second homes being set up in the city. Although English is the international language of the air, BEA encouraged its pilots to learn some German in order to be able to make announcements to the passengers. Predictably enough, this soon led to some schoolboy howlers. On receiving a cold and foggy forecast for Templehof, one captain was emboldened to announce that the conditions at destination were '*kalt und mistig*.' The door to the cockpit was flung open to reveal the German senior stewardess doubled over in the forward galley.

'*Kapitan*,' she managed to splutter, 'You have just told the passengers that the weather in Berlin is shitty!'

Mind you, he could not be faulted on accuracy.

Viscount taxiing in at Renfrew in the '60s.

Templehof itself was relatively close to the boundary between East and West Berlin. When landing on the westerly runway, therefore, we actually overflew part of the East. The contrast between the two parts of the city could not have been starker. West Berlin was a blaze of lights and neon, busy with cars and people. By comparison, East Berlin seemed like a ghost town with dimly lit, half-deserted streets in which only the odd car was to be seen.

Back in London it was soon brought home to me that those BEA pilots who had never flown in Scotland had led a relatively sheltered life. Early one breezy morning I reported for a return trip to Birmingham. In those pre-computer days, I got on with the co-pilot's job of calculating fuel required and maximum permissible take-off weight while my captain went to Met briefing. A few minutes later he returned, announcing,

'You can forget that – we're not going!'

'Why not?' I inquired in some surprise.

'Crosswinds,' he replied. 'It's 250 degrees at twenty-five knots (28 mph).'

The main runway at Birmingham had a heading of 340 at the time, so the wind was indeed at right angles to the runway giving a crosswind component of the full twenty-five knots. However, that was within the Viscount's limit of thirty knots (35mph).

'But they have a runway 25,' (i.e. straight into wind) I protested.

'Too short for a Viscount,' he riposted.

It was in fact not much shorter than the main runway at 1,400 metres. Perfectly acceptable for a Viscount with a brisk headwind component.

By contrast, some months later I found myself arriving at Glasgow where the surface wind was gusting over forty knots (46 mph). Crossing the tarmac I bumped into a familiar figure in the shape of Ralph Landells, one of the captains I had flown with on Dakotas but who had now also moved on to Viscounts.

'Hi Ralph, where are you off to?'

'Round the Hebs.'

(i.e. Renfrew–Benbecula–Stornoway–Inverness–Stornoway–Benbecula–Renfrew)

'Must be a bit rough at Benbecula today?'

'As a matter of fact, it is. 290/60 knots, gusting 80. But, being Benbecula, it also has a 500 foot cloud base!'

Benbecula is one of the few places in Europe where low cloud and hurricane force winds might be found simultaneously. Furthermore the only letdown procedure was on runway 25; clearly impossible to land on with a crosswind component varying from 42 to 56 knots (48–64 mph).

'Fortunately,' continued Ralph, 'that is straight down runway 29.'

The old runway 29, long since closed, was approximately 1,000 meters long. No problem with a headwind of 70 mph but to land on it would involve making an instrument approach to runway 25, breaking off when visual and making a low level circuit in hurricane force winds with all their associated turbulence.

'Are you going?'

'Oh, yes!'

I had to laugh. No one could have raised an eyebrow if Ralph had cancelled the service but the old Scottish spirit of 'the show must go on' was obviously still alive and well. He was contemplating six sectors in conditions which would have kept even old-school island ferry skippers stormbound. It was obvious that through limited exposure to strong winds, many London-based pilots had considerably less confidence in crosswind situations than the battle-hardened Renfrew veterans.

I had managed to find some digs in Richmond with a splendid landlady whose glamorous dress sense and blonde hair testified to a life spent in show business. Jane Shaw's speciality act had involved using yards of assorted fabrics to create stylish dresses using her daughter as a model. Her husband Ed Shore claimed to be the first musician to have used an electric guitar in Britain.

Richmond and Twickenham, being still affordable at the time, were favourite nesting places for single airline pilots and cabin crew. As a result there were frequent weekend parties in the area. One such was still in full swing about one o'clock of a Sunday morning when there was a heavy knock on the door. It was opened to reveal the full majesty of the law in the shape of one of the police constables who used to patrol on the mopeds that had become known as 'noddy bikes'.

'Good morning sir, there has been a bit of a complaint about the noise,'

'Terribly sorry, officer, we'll reduce it at once and apologies to the good citizens we have disturbed.'

'Very good, sir.'

'Don't suppose you'd like a drink, yourself?'

With a practised swipe of the hand he removed his helmet.

'Don't mind if I do, sir!'

A week later at a similar occasion but different venue, another heavy knock announced a repeat visit from the law.

'Good morning, sir, there has been a bit of a complaint about...'

'Don't muck about, Gwyn, come in and have a drink!'

Richmond at the time was hardly a crime spot so our new found Welsh friend had found the best way to while away the boredom of his patrol was to cruise around listening for sounds of revelry. Experience had shown him that guilty attempts to curry favour with the law often resulted in invitations to join the fun. On this occasion he made his excuses after a few beers and disappeared, only to return about twenty minutes later accompanied by his sergeant!

There was one flat in Twickenham shared by three rather attractive BEA stewardesses. It must be remembered that the job in those days was still regarded as one of the most exciting and glamorous for young women. Despite the fact that their maximum period of employment in BEA was ten years and married women were ineligible, competition was fierce for vacancies in the big airlines. In the middle of the night, our trio discovered to their horror that their flat had been invaded by a hamster belonging to their neighbour's little lad. In panic they rang the police. When the emergency was announced on police radio, it is said that three squad cars and two motor bikes turned up to deal with the incident.

These were the days before breathalysers and we thought nothing of driving home after a night's partying. BEA even had its own club on the north side of Heathrow where crew could drop in after flying and have a couple of pints in uniform in yet another brave attempt to counter the dreaded effects of airborne dehydration. That is not quite as frivolous as it sounds. In the 60s the Ruffell-Smith investigation into pilot fatigue levels revealed, inter-alia, that humidity in the Viscount's pressurised cabin could drop close to zero. That could have quite unpleasant physiological repercussions such as the body re-absorbing its own urine. As noted previously in the Transport Command section, some continental airlines had happily served wine to their pilots with in-flight meals. Their cultures could not conceive of a meal being complete without it. The practice was only just disappearing. Pilot Union BALPA maintains that chronic fatigue is more dangerous to safety than any evidence of alcohol abuse.

Although I was happy in my digs in Sheen Road under the indulgent supervision of Jane Shaw, the notoriously arctic winter of 1962-3 brought home the disadvantages of a lack of central heating. The solitary bathroom had no form of heating and hot water came from a gas geyser. It was common to see ice on the *inside* of windows and having a bath was something of an ordeal. The technique was to remain fully dressed until the bath was filled to the requisite level before ripping off clothes and leaping into the safety of the warm water. The worst was still to come for the cooling water made it inevitable that eventually the freezing air had to be braved while drying off.

As a Viscount First Officer my salary had almost doubled to just over £2,000 per annum. Emboldened by these riches, I started looking around for a place of my own. Eventually I found a very desirable centrally-heated, two-bedroom maisonette on a new Wates estate at Ham, halfway between Richmond and Kingston. Thanks to a 90% mortgage I could now afford its price of £3,950, although colleagues sucked their teeth.

'You'll never get your money back!'

As the workhorse of the airline, the Viscount was instrumental in introducing me to the skies and airports of Europe and beyond. English is the international language of aviation but national languages can also be used within their home boundaries. Back then, some countries were more chauvinistic than others in exercising this right with a consequent lack of fluency in English.

We arrived at the old airport in Mallorca one day simultaneously with two other aircraft. This was unusual for the island was yet to experience the explosion in tourists which made it the top holiday destination of the Mediterranean. In the absence of radar, the controller was ejected out of his comfort zone by this level of congestion and virtually gave up. We three liaised with each other and, once in visual contact, arranged a suitable orderly procession towards the landing runway.

If anything the smaller airports in France were worse if one departed from standard phraseology. There was a four sector day trip to Bordeaux and Biarritz. Captain Benny Yorston and I had just departed Bordeaux on the second sector when a calm American voice came over the airwaves:

'Bordeaux, this is XXX012, request a heading for a straight in approach, runway 11 at Bordeaux.'

No reply, so the message was repeated.

'Aircraft calling Bordeaux, say again.'

'Bordeaux this is XXX012, I estimate my position as twenty miles due west of Bordeaux, I have zero fuel, repeat zero fuel, request a heading for a straight in approach runway 11 at Bordeaux!'

With any competent controller, such a message would have resulted in the unfortunate aircraft being given every possible assistance and cooperation. To our stunned horror, the controller proceeded to give a routine weather report for Bordeaux, including the information that the wind was westerly at twenty knots.

'Sir, I say again, can I have a heading for a straight in approach runway 11?'

'012, Bordeaux, the runway in use at Bordeaux is 29!'

'Sir, I am not really interested in your runway in use. I have zero fuel. If my engines stop now, I will be landing straight ahead in the water. Can I have a heading for a straight in approach?'

'We are only trying to be the Tower!'

'Heading please?'

'012, Bordeaux, are you receiving the Bordeaux VOR?'

'Affirmative'

'On what radial of the Bordeaux VOR are you?'

'291'

'Ah – Roger! Steer 111 degrees for Bordeaux.'

We could not believe our ears. The 291 radial indicated that the stranger was indeed slightly north of due west from Bordeaux but all the controller had done was to give this pilot in dire emergency the reciprocal bearing which he would already have known. However, at this point we had to transfer to the Biarritz frequency, desperate to discover how this tragicomedy was going to play out. When we landed back at Bordeaux on the return, we were relieved to see what looked like an ex-Pan Am Boeing Stratocruiser sitting on the tarmac. When our ground engineer came aboard we quizzed him eagerly on the course of events.

'It was quite dramatic,' he said. 'He touched down on Runway 11 with a twenty knot tailwind, rolled to the end of the runway and all four engines ran down!'

The Stratocruiser apparently now belonged to an Israeli charter airline and had just crossed the Atlantic from America. The Strat had a characteristically nose up attitude on the ground and we reckoned that, with the lower nose-down attitude on the approach, the last few drops of gasoline were feeding from the bottom of the tanks into the engines. Once the pilot flared for the landing there was nothing left. You cannot cut the Atlantic crossing any finer than that! While the eventual outcome was successful, it was small thanks to the controller. Nowadays, the general standard of European Air Traffic Control is excellent. Some years later when one of our aeroplanes had a major emergency over Paris, it was allocated its own discrete radio frequency and a controller who spoke perfect English.

There was one other memorable incident of the time which nearly brought my nascent airline career to a premature conclusion. I had taken myself off to Mallorca for a bit of leave. At that time the island was just beginning its rise to most popular tourist destination in the Mediterranean. Puerto Andraitx was still a little port with local fishing boats lining the wharf in a bay nowadays full of yachts. A lunch at one of the pier side cafes still sticks in my memory as one of the great meals of my life. For what seemed ridiculously few pesetas, it consisted simply of a bowl of prawns fresh from the boat alongside with a garlic mayonnaise washed down with a nicely chilled bottle of dry white.

When the time came to abandon the Spanish sun I was delighted to find that the Iberia London flight was operated by a Caravelle – the twin-jet that was starting a revolution in short-haul services. As we cruised at 31,000 feet towards the Pyrenees, I requested a cockpit visit. The captain's grasp of English was rudimentary but he did his best to explain some of the novel features of his new toy.

Suddenly, he exclaimed in Spanish and pointed ahead to the right. Out there was another Caravelle which had just crossed our track at the same level. Even as we looked there was a bump as we flew through his slipstream. It was the flight from Barcelona to Paris which had been cleared to the same level as us. We had missed each other by a couple of hundred yards.

This was the sort of incident that all the safety procedures should have made impossible. For any pilot with fluent English an official report of Air Miss would have been filed immediately with Air Traffic Control and would have been taken extremely seriously. But in Spain, as in France, maximum use was made of the concession that the national language could be used as an alternative to English. It was clear that the Captain's command of international standard language was such that he was unable to report properly the seriousness of the incident. It was the closest I had yet come to an early demise.

Although nowadays nearly all airline operations are closely supervised by Air Traffic control, considerably more pilot discretion was allowed back in the 60s. In good weather pilots were often permitted to climb in accordance with Visual Flight Rules which allowed them to take responsibility for their own separation from other aircraft or high ground. Turin lies very close to the Alps and so northbound flights had to climb to a safe altitude above the airfield before setting course. One clear winter morning, my bold captain requested permission to save time by climbing visually, knowing that we would have achieved our cruising level of 18,000 feet before we reached Mont Blanc. Now mountains and clouds always look higher as you initially approach them. Halfway through the climb it looked as though we were heading towards an impenetrable wall of granite-cored snow, shining brightly in the morning sun. At this point the senior steward entered the flight deck. It was the first time I had actually seen someone's jaw physically drop.

But the Alps had to be treated with respect. Milan Linate and Malpensa had similar, if less restrictive, safe height-gaining procedures. We came out of the latter one morning in a heavy-laden Viscount 802 (i.e. with less powerful engines). This time it was cloudy but we climbed without incident to the 18,000 feet level which should give a safety margin of over 2,000 feet for the transit of Mont Blanc's 15,777 foot peak. However, as we approached the Alps our speed started to fall off and it became impossible to maintain height. It was necessary to make an emergency request to turn away from the mountains in order to regain speed and height and climb to the next

The rare sight of four Viscount 800s at Kirkwall in April 1982 as BA mounted a special expedition to mark the end of the Viscount era. By then the more powerful 806 models had been re-engined to 802 standard.

higher level of 20,000. Only then could we resume the northerly flight. It transpired that the north wind over the Alps was much stronger than forecast and thus was creating a massive downdraft on the southerly side of the mountains.

Modern jets cruise in the 30,000–40,000 feet range so their safety margins are considerably more generous. However, there were some plus factors to the lower cruising levels used by propjets such as the Viscount and Vanguard. As the route over Geneva and Turin on the airway lay close to the summit of Mont Blanc, crossing the Alps on a sunny day could be an awe-inspiring experience. Despite the safety height giving a clearance of more than 2,000 feet, it often felt as though you could lean out and touch the peak.

I had rapidly found myself at home in the Viscount – particularly in its more powerful 806 version. To my great delight I was eventually selected to undertake some training duties on ground courses for those converting to the fleet. It was the best of all possible worlds; flying a modern turbojet and also exercising some of the teaching skills of my original career choice.

The Comet

As air travel started to expand in the 50s, BEA realised that a bigger aircraft would be required to succeed the Viscount. Although passenger jets had entered the aviation scene with the ill-fated deHavilland Comet 1, it was initially thought (quite correctly) that jet speeds would be of little advantage on short sectors and the economics could not be justified. Accordingly, an order was placed for the Vickers Vanguard, powered by four Rolls Royce Tyne turboprops and capable of carrying 139 passengers at about 400 mph.

deHavilland Comet 4b. Arguably the most
beautiful commercial jet of all time. © *BEA*

Unfortunately, the Vanguard was plagued by early production problems, particularly with the engine compressors which provided the pressurisation. In 1960, Vickers set up a proving flight to the Middle East with BEA senior pilots, Captain A.S. Johnson who was to be the flight manager and Captain Ron Gillman who was to be the senior training manager. As nearly every sector involved an engine shut down, it is alleged that at the end of the tour Ron Gilman innocently enquired of the Vickers pilot,

'Now, when can we see some four-engine landings?'

The consequent delays to entry into service were bad news for Vickers. Suddenly, competitors in Europe were flying the jet French, Caravelle. Fortunately, deHavilland had completely redesigned their early Comets to produce the Mark 4 version for BOAC. On 4 October 1958 they cheekily operated the first jet passenger services between London and New York, beating Pan American's 707 by a few weeks. The 4c was a longer range version thanks to extra pinion fuel tanks on the wings.

Long term, BEA planned to introduce the three-engined DH 121 jet which they had tailored to their routes as the Trident (eventually built by Hawker Siddley). As an emergency measure, they hurriedly ordered seven of deHavilland's shorter haul model, the Comet 4b. With a shorter wingspan and longer fuselage, it was arguably the most beautiful commercial jet of all time. Eventually it became necessary to increase that order to fourteen. BEA's first jet service was between London and Tel Aviv on 1 April 1960, more than ten months before the much-delayed Vanguard carried its first scheduled commercial passengers from London to Paris on 22 February 1961.

The Comet was designed for a crew of two pilots and a flight engineer. BEA had no flight engineers but did have ground engineering cover throughout the short haul network. It was decided that the third crew member should be another pilot so that he would be better able to monitor the two up front. In practice, the two first officers alternated their duties on the flight engineer's panel. While this meant their opportunities for sharing the flying were halved, the experience of operating the complex hydraulic, electrical and pressurisation systems of the Comet was to prove invaluable to future understanding of technical mysteries in other aircraft.

Naturally there was great competition to crew this supremely elegant premier aircraft of the fleet. As promotion was by seniority, it attracted the longest-serving captains and co-pilots – with the proviso that the latter had to have been assessed as 'Above Average' on their six-monthly competency checks.

While it was very exciting to join the Comet ground technical course in January 1963, the lecture/book-based courses of the time made for a protracted experience. It was the end of March before the great day came that made all the academic slog worthwhile. In the modern era, it is possible for experienced pilots to learn correct landing technique in super-sophisticated simulators before they fly the aeroplane itself for the first time. Back then, BEA's Comet simulator had a limited range of movement and very little sensation of a real aeroplane. Truth be told, even the modern all-moving simulators never fully convinced me that they could replicate the feel of an aeroplane. Certainly in 1963 we were still required to spend some days handling the real machine before we could be allowed into the pilot's seat on a passenger service.

Day one of the syllabus involved exploring the flight range from low speed stalls at one end to high speed mach buffet at the other. Our first realisation of the extent to which our aviation horizons were literally being broadened was when we departed Heathrow and were handed over to London Air Traffic Control. The most convenient place for these exercises was over the North Sea – then a much quieter aviation environment than is the case today. When asked by the radar controller what sort of area we might need, our training captain boldly requested the use of airspace between Clacton and Newcastle.

The aeroplane proved to be delightful to handle and easy to land, although not quite so flattering and forgiving as the Sud Aviation Caravelle. Early models of the French aeroplane had a fuselage nose section influenced by the Comet and had a similar undercarriage arrangement but with the crucial difference that, on approach, the bogies trailed with the rear wheels lower. This seemed to enable the aircraft to subside gently onto the ground on touchdown, making for some very smooth arrivals. On the Comet the forward wheels on the bogie were slightly lower on the approach and it was usually necessary to make more of a flare to ensure the rear wheels touched first.

The smaller French aircraft also made do with two Rolls Royce Avon engines mounted at the rear. This made for a quieter cabin and a more economical operation. The Comet's four Avons gave an exhilarating performance but noise levels were high aft of the wing. So whereas on Viscounts and Vanguards the first class cabin was at the rear to avoid propeller noise, the opposite philosophy prevailed on jets. The thirstiness of the four Avons would give a modern accountant sleepless nights, but in those days aviation kerosene was still a very cheap fuel.

After proving we could actually land the aeroplane, we were released for the line training phase of the syllabus. Converting pilots have to fly many sectors under supervision by training captains before they are deemed competent to be part of a normal crew. On the more junior fleets this had generally been a very pleasant experience with our mentors keen to pass on to us the benefits of their much greater experience. Comets provided a rude awakening as we encountered for the first time the most senior captains in the corporation and a very different approach. Some had come from long haul aviation when BEA was formed and, with a few honourable exceptions, often had an extremely old-fashioned attitude to training. Truth to tell, there was little attempt at training other than criticism.

'You prove to me you can do it; I point out where you go wrong!'

Now there is little point in telling an experienced pilot that he has done something wrong (he knows that) unless you can diagnose why things went wrong and, more importantly, suggest what needs to be done to improve.

The cockpit management philosophy created further problems. Both co-pilots were usually senior first officers, which means that they held the Air Transport Pilot's Licence that qualified them to act in command. They were also mostly ex-RAF or Navy with a considerable amount of jet time. Captains, on the other hand, were generally much older and converting to their first jet. Despite that, the captain was expected to exercise tight control over his men rather than rely on sensible support from them. As a result, the pressure on captains during conversion was even more intense than on co-pilots. The more verbose and thick-skinned seemed to survive the experience better than those who might be instinctive aeroplane handlers but were not so good at issuing streams of instructions to perfectly able team members while still having to concentrate on acquiring new skills.

In the year of my conversion, one of the latter group suffered a multiple heart attack while another committed suicide. Another much respected training captain from Viscounts nearly suffered a nervous breakdown. There was little doubt in my mind that the stress of the conversion course was responsible. Of course, some trainers were excellent but there were sufficient of the others for Comet training flight to become known as the 'Gestapo'. To understand why the poisonous atmosphere was so counter-productive, you have only to realise that pilots operate on self-confidence. Once that self-belief is destroyed by niggling criticism without any compensating recognition of progress it takes much longer to rebuild.

The other shock was to find that approach procedures on our sleek new jet were considerably more long-winded than we had been accustomed to on Viscounts or even Dakotas. In the older aeroplanes we had been keen to exploit any opportunity to operate more efficiently by seeking shorter routings or permission to maintain speed as long as possible. Perhaps as a concession to more senior captains without previous jet experience, the Comet training establishment's pedestrian approach had us slowing to approach speeds with flaps and even gear down with over twenty miles to run. I watched in disbelief as Viscounts whistled past us and consequently achieved earlier slots in the landing sequence. Co-pilots on conversion didn't suffer

Comet 4b cockpit. Moisture frozen on the inside skin in flight tended to melt during descent. The consequent drips in the cockpit encouraged the wearing of jackets! The Decca navigator display (centre) had a pen which traced out the route on a moving paper roll.

quite as badly as captains because they were regarded as less important. Nevertheless, it was a great sense of relief that we were eventually cleared as competent to operate on the line as co-pilots and flight engineers.

Fortunately, it took only one flight as a member of an ordinary line crew to reassure me that life could still be fun. It may even have been deliberate policy by the office staff to crew those newly escaped from the grim clutches of training flight together with some of the captains least likely to pay much attention to excessively cautious procedures. Captain TR (Panda) Watson, was certainly one of those. Returning from Milan Linate we were encouraged to keep the speed up and Panda took full advantage to the extent that we were still doing over 300 knots as we turned onto the final approach for the westerly runway at Heathrow. It was my turn to operate the flight engineer's panel and the co-pilot was racing through the extensive Comet approach and landing checklist. He had no sooner completed it than his captain said, 'I say, old boy, why don't you land it!' The startled co-pilot dropped the check list and grabbed the control column while Panda carried on a cheerful flow of chat. Not getting much in the way of reply, he said, 'Terribly sorry, old chap, concentrating are we?' Meanwhile, behind them on the panel I was killing myself laughing. Life in this fleet was going to be all right.

In fact, the way of life on Comets proved to be very pleasant indeed. The aeroplane itself was a pilot's dream, being blessed with pleasant handling and a superabundance of power for its weight. Thanks to its long-haul pedigree, it also had the ability to carry plenty of fuel. That precious commodity was still so cheap that ample reserves could be carried to cater for all the vagaries of European weather. Thus we had the luxury by today's standards of carrying enough spare fuel into London to have the ever-reliable Prestwick as the usual alternate. [It is a legal requirement for a commercial flight to carry sufficient fuel to fly to a suitable alternate with acceptable weather and be able to hold for 45 minutes. Accountants nowadays require the alternate to be the closest possible.]

Air traffic control was improving throughout the network – with only the occasional glitch. The weather report we picked up from Barcelona approach control one fine morning promised little problem with no low cloud and a north easterly wind of 20 knots straight down Runway 07. We duly made our approach and all went well till we whizzed across the threshold of the runway at what seemed an unusually high rate. Fortunately the Comet had excellent brakes but as we slowed towards the end of the runway we passed a windsock fully extended. Just what you might expect with a wind of 20 knots but indicating that instead of a headwind we had landed with a tailwind.

'Barcelona can you check your surface wind? This windsock is indicating south westerly.'

'Standby.'

After a few moments embarrassed silence:

'Correction. Our anemometer is broken. We estimate the wind as 250/20 knots!'

In other words we had landed at a speed well above our permitted tailwind for the runway with a touchdown speed some 45 mph higher than we had been anticipating. We were lucky that the runway was long enough to save us from an over-run.

As previously mentioned, our routes were not confined to Europe despite the title of the airline. Athens became a secondary hub airport for BEA. From there, services radiated out to Istanbul and Ankara, Cairo, Tel Aviv and Beirut. In the 60s, the latter was still one of the pleasure spots of the Mediterranean with good hotels, restaurants and an active night life. It was possible to ski in the mountains in the morning and swim in the sea in the afternoon. The sectors from there to Bahrain, Kuwait and Doha were much easier hops for the Comet than they had been for the Viscount. Beirut–London was the one sector where we were actually in direct competition with BOAC Comet 4s. We did find it amusing that the BOAC timetable claimed a shorter schedule time for the Beirut–London sector than ours. In fact, the clipped wing BEA Comet 4b had the higher cruise speed of .79 Mach against the Comet 4's .76.

Some of our flights operated on contract to Cyprus Airways before that airline had its own fleet. This caused BOAC to accuse BEA of using the arrangement to trespass on routes east of the island they considered part of their empire. Before the Turkish invasion of Cyprus in1974, Nicosia was a favourite destination and the whole island was open for exploration. The crew hotel was the Dome in Kyrenia north of the Troodos mountains where temperatures in summer made for more comfortable nights. On Cyprus Airways flights we carried local Greek-speaking cabin crew, male and female. Cypriot society was still very conservative when it came to dealing with the free-wheeling sun-seekers of the new jet age. Although the cabin crew had to night-stop in Athens, they stayed in a different hotel and never socialised with the pilots. Despite their impeccable behaviour it was considered rather scandalous in Cypriot villages that the stewardesses spent nights away from home unchaperoned.

Cypriot sherry was still popular in the UK and was available in its home island in quantity at knockdown prices. It became a crew tradition to pick it up in five-litre, wicker-covered jars. It is true that the dry variety was a little sour and the sweet was somewhat sickly. The solution was to mix the two and there was a general consensus that a blend of three litres of dry with two of sweet was about right. Cypriot brandy was not much more expensive so it was not long before the more adventurous were mixing two litres of brandy with three of sherry. This lethal cocktail could still be passed off as sherry to Customs and was guaranteed to get any crew party off to a flying start.

During the period when EOKA was still actively pursuing the dream of a union with Greece, BEA services seemed to be strangely unaffected. Rumour later suggested that this might have been because our station superintendent at Nicosia was an officer in EOKA. However, any resultant complacency was cruelly shattered. On 10 October 1967, it had been my pleasure to fly the Nicosia–Athens leg of a service to London. Two days later, on the 12th, the news came through that another Comet, G-ARCO, had crashed in the Mediterranean with the loss of all on board. As it was operating Cyprus Airways Flight 284 the pilots were BEA while the cabin attendants were Cypriot. A painstaking investigation was later to prove that a bomb had exploded under a passenger seat. Apparently there had been a rumour that General Grivas was to be on board. Grivas, a Cypriot who had become a general in the Greek Army, was EOKA's leader.

Olympic Comet operating a BEA domestic service at the old terminal at Edinburgh. The tiny red square which identified it as a BEA service is only just visible at the rear passenger door.

The bomb explosion was in the forward first class compartment and caused an explosive decompression of the aircraft. The crew initiated the correct emergency drill which required the crew to don oxygen masks and commence an immediate descent using the powerful airbrakes at full speed of 320 knots. Oxygen masks would also have deployed for the passengers, During this dive the aircraft disintegrated but the simpler recorders of the time did not record the succession of events. The cruising level was only 29,000 feet, which is not so critical from an oxygen point of view as the usual 33,000. We wondered whether a gentler descent technique might have permitted it to survive but there was no way of checking this. We mourned the loss of our colleagues and the other innocent victims on board but our flights went on.

The only other European airline operating the Comet 4b was Olympic Airlines in Greece. BEA had agreed a technical consortium with them so that if necessary they could use our aeroplanes and we could use theirs. Some worried that this was conferring respectability on a small airline competitor whose fleet was still piston engined. It did lead to some bizarre sights such as an Olympic Comet operating British domestic flights. Occasionally, some of BEA's customers could be rather alarmed to find a foreign aircraft operating their service and had to be persuaded that the crew were in fact British. However, given that Athens was BEA's busiest

Comet transit destination after Heathrow, the consortium did make a certain amount of sense.

The city of Athens was thus a major social hotspot for BEA crews. At any one time there might be three or four crews night-stopping in the old art nouveau Acropole Palace Hotel. The pound was still so strong that one of them was sufficient for a good night out in the many tavernas and night clubs. Morale on board was considerably enhanced by the fact that BEA still operated a policy of rostering pilots and cabin staff as one crew. Socialising together on night stops made for a much better *esprit de corps* on duty. Later power-building within the cabin crew empire saw an insistence that they have control of separate rosters. This break in the link with pilots led to ridiculous situations to the extent that it was possible to fly with three different cabin crews in one four-sector day. There was a consequent deterioration in communication and empathy between pilots and flight attendants from which BA suffers to this day.

Back in the 60s, for those fortunate enough to have a slip day in Athens, Glyfada beach resort became the rendezvous of choice for sun worshippers. Aristotle Onassis's yacht *Christina* could be seen at anchor and his private pilot often joined the airline group. For culture vultures, the National Archaeological Museum lay just across the street and opportunities for tours by coach or by ferry from Piraeus were endless.

One slip day in 1963 some of us took a coach tour to Delphi. While we pored over the ruins, the *Christina* suddenly appeared in the bay below. Shortly afterwards, who should appear at the site but Jackie, wife of US President John F Kennedy. She was accompanied by her younger sister, Princess Lee Radziwill. I was struck by the physical resemblance that both had to Maria Callas, then Onassis's mistress. At the time in Britain the Kennedys were still the golden couple and John F himself was regarded as the white hope for the western world. The Americans on the tour bus soon disillusioned us. According to them (presumably Republicans) it had been an open secret that the Kennedy marriage was in trouble before he was elected although it had continued for political expediency. Later that year, I was with a group of friends on my way to the Albert Hall for the BEA Annual Ball when the taxi driver broke the world-shaking news that Kennedy had been shot. It was no surprise when Jackie took up with Onassis and eventually married him. Callas was devastated – but revisionist history alleges that Lee was also furious because she too had had an affair with Onassis.

Hotels throughout Europe were only too pleased to have a steady income from night-stopping crews. The truth was that tourist air traffic was still in its infancy. Passengers dressed in their smartest clothes to go flying and the First Class cabin was a haunt of the rich and famous. Film stars interested in technology such as Danny Kaye and Peter Sellers were keen to visit the flight deck. Members of the royal family were often to be seen on board on private trips.

The first class cabin was immediately aft of the cockpit and BEA's catering regularly included lobster, caviar and, of course, champagne. Comet cabin crew were specially selected and noted for their ability to deliver a first class service on some very short sectors. The longest was the direct flight from Athens to London at about three hours and forty-five minutes. A good cabin crew would ensure that their first class passengers could enjoy a leisurely lunch occupying most of that time.

On the other hand, I once flew as a passenger back to London on Olympic's parallel service. Less than an hour after take-off, the lunch service was over and done with. The cabin crew then disappeared from sight for most of the rest of the flight.

Comets operated regular services to capital cities behind the iron curtain. Given the political atmosphere of the time, the service to Moscow had a particular frisson to it. Apart from technical differences, such as the use of metres instead of feet for flight levels, it was necessary to carry an interpreter for communication with Russian controllers. Airways were only ten kilometres wide (compared to ten miles in the west) and guidance was by medium frequency radio beacons which had limited range and were notoriously affected by bad weather. There was also an unspoken threat that if we strayed outside the airway we might be intercepted by fighters.

Comet 4b at Berlin Tempelhof, '60s.

Life got even more complicated when the Comet was introduced on the German Internal services along the corridors to Berlin in competition with Pan Am's Boeing 727s. Thanks to the restrictions to flight below 10,000 feet still imposed by the Russians, the aeroplane was operating well below its comfort zone. It was not just that the voracious Avon engines were even more thirsty at these altitudes but we also lost our ability to soar above any bad weather enroute. Fortunately for the Avons, aviation fuel was still dirt cheap before the price explosion of the seventies but the German summer is a season of high temperatures and thunderstorms.

Our ability to manoeuvre to avoid the latter was severely restricted by the narrowness of the corridors. The temperatures posed further problems in terms of passenger comfort for the Comet was not fitted with that Auxiliary Power Unit which, apart from supplying electrical power, air-conditions modern aircraft on the ground. Before take-off with a full load the cabin could very quickly transform itself into a sweaty sauna. Unfortunately the shortness of the sectors and the warmer air at low levels made it very difficult to cool the cabin before arrival at destination. The very act of pressurising the aircraft in itself tended to introduce a heating effect through compression of the air as it maintained the effective cabin height close to ground level. Flight time was insufficient for cabin temperature to be reduced to normal.

My sectors as flight engineer enabled me to experiment with a different technique to deal with the problem. Selecting an initial cabin height of 8,000 feet (normal for a long high level sector) reduced the compression effect without having too much effect on passenger ears. As the cabin cooled I could then gently reduce cabin height so that the more critical descent profile could be accomplished at a rate comfortable for the passengers. You could rely on the German cabin crew to keep you informed if you got it wrong!

While it was true that BEA's Comet cabin crew were selected from those with the highest assessments, the 'grass is greener' syndrome often led politically incorrect pilots to speculate wistfully on the exotic attraction of cabin staff from other airlines. To be truthful, I only remember one experience when such odious comparisons seemed well founded. In those less frenetic times, schedules often allowed time for lunch on foreign turnarounds. Helsinki was one of those and on this occasion we noted that a Pan Am Boeing 707 was already on the tarmac.

Halfway through the feast, a sudden hush fell over the room and we looked round to see that a small gaggle had just entered. In the middle of the group were two stunning blue-eyed blondes whose sky-blue Pan Am uniforms looked as though

Comet 4B G-APMB on an early service to Frankfurt in 1961.

they had been sculpted to their perfect figures. Wistful wasn't in it. There were men in the restaurant whose jaws were hanging open with their forks arrested in mid air. At this moment our local traffic officer arrived with some information for the captain.

'Have you seen Pan Am!' someone stuttered.

'Don't worry,' he smiled, 'They are making a film. The nearest one is Miss Finland 1966, the other Miss Finland 1967!'

The Tiger Club

*I*t felt like a real privilege to crew the Comet despite spending half of all flights as flight engineer. The more senior captains were also likely to be less generous with the amount of flying they offered to co-pilots. Whereas we had been accustomed to sharing the flying on a fifty-fifty basis the best we could now hope for was less than a quarter. The consolation was the feeling that we were operating the best aeroplane in the world. My progress was recognised when I was selected to become a training first officer. This involved supervising converting first officers on their operation of the flight engineer's panel and acting as monitor while they were being introduced to co-pilot duties.

While I was enjoying my airline flying, there were drawbacks to being a co-pilot. The need to adjust to the whims and eccentricities of individual captains made a grasp of psychology an unwritten but key component of the job description. For those of us from a forces background, deference to authority was an ingrained part of our being. Even so, it is also part of a co-pilot's make-up to assume that his natural brilliance is only being constrained by the dozy old captain in the left-hand seat.

It did not help that some of our bosses could hardly claim to have gained their position through merit. A classical example occurred when I tried to do something about some of the failures in cross-wind landing technique I had observed on the line. The procedure I had absorbed on the Dakota worked just as well on the Comet, as indeed it did on all the other aeroplanes I had flown from the Tiger Moth upwards. Full of missionary zeal, I approached my training manager with the suggestion that the technique should be taught officially.

'It would not work on a Comet,' he replied dismissively, 'the yaw dampers would cancel out the yaw.'

(Yaw dampers were fitted to eliminate a rolling or yawing instability which affected some jet aircraft).

'It does work,' I riposted. 'I've done it.'

'You've got no bloody business to have done it,' he blustered. 'I'll send you back for further base training.'

Bear in mind that at the time I was one of his training first officers, regularly receiving above average assessments on refresher training. That sort of arrogance was typical of the bullying attitudes which had blighted initial conversion to the Comet for so many.

For alternative therapy I was fortunate to be introduced to a flying club at Redhill which actually encouraged hot-blooded young aviators to do crazy things with aeroplanes. The Tiger Club was the brainchild of Norman Jones, an amiable if occasionally explosive eccentric. The club fleet was a mixture of deHavilland Tiger Moths, Belgian Stampes, Druine Turbulents and a few individual one-offs. Some

Air race practice in Turbulent G-APNZ in 1961.

French Jodels acted as support aircraft or catered for those interested in touring.

Flying members had to have a minimum of a hundred hours experience but were also required to pass a handling check on the open cockpit Tiger Moth which gave the club its name. The result was a delightful mixture of enthusiasts drawn from all classes and all sections of the aviation community. Private pilots, members of the aristocracy, commercial and military pilots were united in their wish to do something adventurous with aeroplanes whether it be aerobatics, formation flying, racing or anything else that seemed like fun.

Every summer the club ran six or seven air displays modelled on the barnstorming of the inter-war years. The Volkswagen-engined Druine Turbulent was allegedly non-aerobatic but four of them could put on a spirited display within a very compact airspace. The repertoire included a tail chase, cutting paper streamers with the propellers and flying under a string held between two poles about twenty yards apart. Seen from the air this gate looked ludicrously inadequate but the pilots just aimed for the middle and relied on the fact that the aircraft head-on profile was smaller than the gap. By comparison, flying under a bridge (which the public would regard as foolhardy in the extreme) is a doddle.

The Turbulent was my introduction to display flying. This tiny, open-cockpit single-seater was so like donning a pair of wings that on my first flight I flew around giggling inanely to myself at the sheer impudence of the concept. Eventually I was accepted as a member of the team. We would fly to our air display venues in a loose gaggle, taking advantage of any opportunity to indulge in a bit of unauthorised low flying. Compared with the organised formality of commercial flying it was therapeutic to climb into an open cockpit non-radio aeroplane, navigate by map to a strange airfield, work out the circuit and landing pattern from visual clues alone and then so arrange the landing that you ended up at the closest point to the petrol pumps.

We were returning to Redhill from one Sunday display in 1961 when I became aware that I was having some trouble keeping up with the other Turbulents. Gradually the Volkswagen engine got rougher until I decided it would be safer to land in a field than run the risk of complete failure. I selected a very promising grass area conveniently close to a major road. However, on final approach it became clear that the field sloped downhill which was not the ideal prospect for an aircraft without brakes. I decided to climb away and look for a safer alternative but the engine died when I tried to open the throttle. Touchdown was fine but the Turb then trundled sedately downhill till it dipped into a ditch at the end with its nose in the hedge. There was a farmhouse nearby where I knocked on the door with the classic line, 'I have just crashed in your field.'

*A four-plane Turbulent formation appeared at the
Farnborough air show on public days in the '60s.*

The farm actually belonged to Sir Ivor Griffiths, an ENT surgeon of the old school famous in particular for his work with opera singers. He accepted the drama with aplomb. Luckily for me his weekend guest was his assistant surgeon at Hammersmith Hospital, Vincent Briffa. Despite my poor choice of field, I had at least picked a farm in Northamptonshire where there was someone actually driving back to London that evening. During the drive to a suitable underground station we discovered a mutual interest in theatre and opera which led to a lifelong friendship.

The novelty of the Turbulent act achieved its proudest recognition in the 60s when we were invited to take part in the Farnborough Air Display on the public open days. From Turbulents the natural progression was to Tiger Moths and Stampes, both classic training biplanes. As well as aerobatics, the Tiger Moth acts included crazy flying and tied together formation. Girlfriends could be found who would be brave enough to endure the 100 mph icy blast involved in standing on the upper wing of a Tiger. There was keen competition to become a member of the display team, not least because practice flying was subsidised and display flying was free.

Unlike the Tiger, the Belgian Stampe has ailerons on both wings. Its superior rate of roll made for a much more versatile aerobatic mount. Nearly all the top

110

British aerobatic pilots of the time were members of the club. The emphasis the RCAF had placed on formation flying paid off as I found a regular slot in the display team. None of these old aeroplanes had radio so all the leader's instructions were relayed by a system of hand signals which probably dated back to WWI.

Air racing was part of the sporting aviation scene although for most it was done on a shoestring. The motley mixture of entrants required that the races were handicap events. Financial rewards there were none so for most of us it was just a bit of fun and another opportunity for some semi-official low flying. My early efforts were in a Turbulent and gradually I worked up to Tiger Moths. The nearest I got to any modest success was when I declared a passenger on the club's venerable Tiger G-ACDC. By managing to persuade the most petite girl I knew to fill the role I was able to take some advantage of the handicap allowance for passenger weight.

Eventually the club trusted me with their most prized possession – the Le Vier Cosmic Wind. This beautiful little racer had an outstanding rate of roll which gave it superb aerobatic potential, while its scimitar prop delivered a remarkable turn of speed from its 90 horse power engine. It was used to open the club displays by roaring in on the dot of three o'clock and pulling up into two vertical rolls to start its routine. So it was with considerable pride and anticipation that I landed the Cosmic in Halfpenny Green airfield for a new air race which had been added to those

The author in close formation in a single seat 'Super' Tiger Moth.

111

organised by the Royal Aeronautical Society. The course involved a turn shortly after take-off but I practised round it on the morning of the race and was happy that I could safely pull a fairly tight turn even before achieving full speed.

By the time of the race briefing a few things had changed. The stewards had belatedly realised that by the time the fast aircraft took off, the early starters would be completing the first lap. So, for separation purposes, they introduced a new turning point (known as a scatter point). Not only was this closer to the end of the runway but it also required a turn of more than 90 degrees. The Cosmic engine was proving reluctant to start when hot. So as second last to get airborne I sat for some time by the starting point with engine running awaiting my turn. In the meantime, unbeknown to me in my non-radio state, the wind had backed and the August afternoon temperature had risen. Just as I was about to roll, someone tapped on the canopy and shouted that there were two slower aeroplanes coming up on the course.

Secret of success in a handicap race: find a petite lady brave enough to be a passenger! Helen and G-ACDC in 1963.

Throttle wide open and off I went. As I banked steeply into the first turn, I looked back over my shoulder for the conflicting traffic. Next thing I knew, I was waking up on the ground and people were trying to pull me out of the cockpit. I could not believe what must have happened.

To this day I have no memory of the last few seconds of that fateful flight. The best I can do is attempt to reconstruct what I think happened. The earlier turn and change in wind direction meant that I hit the turn at a slower speed than on my morning practice. More importantly, while looking back there is a tendency to pull back harder than intended. Stalling speed increases with the amount of g force being pulled and the Cosmic must have shown her resentment by flicking out of the turn.

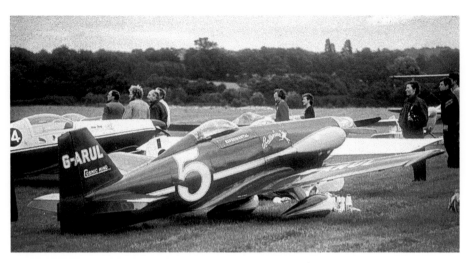

Cosmic Wind at a Redhill display.

The Cosmic Wind required a complete rebuild before she could fly again.

Another piece of the jigsaw fell into place several years later when I spoke for the first time to the pilot of one of the slow aeroplanes I had been hoping to avoid. He said he saw the Cosmic start its take-off roll as he came overhead the field but noticed that, in relation to his wing leading edge, the acceleration did not seem to be smooth. It is more than likely that the engine had overheated on the ground and was not developing its normal power.

The miracle was that I had survived at all after hitting the ground at about 130 mph – and that the aeroplane had not caught fire. True, I was quite badly smashed up with broken tibia and fibula in my right leg, a broken rib and three collapsed lumbar vertebrae. Though I was wearing a full harness, my head had hit the instrument panel and my face needed forty eight stitches. Some of them were in my left eyelid, but by another miracle the eye itself was untouched. Thanks to the collapsed vertebrae I discovered I was two thirds of an inch shorter than I had been. But I had no right to have survived that August bank holiday of 1966, never mind continue to enjoy many years of good health. Those subsequent years have been pure bonus.

Like most accidents, it had come about from a series of factors lining up. Like most accidents, also, the general diagnosis was pilot error. Sadly, nothing was done about the turning point so close to the runway that faster aircraft had to turn around before reaching full flying speed.

Six years later, in the same air race, Prince William of Gloucester and his friend crashed just after takeoff in very similar circumstances. Tragically they were both killed. Prince William was ninth in line to the throne and his cousin Prince Charles named his eldest son William in his memory. Who knows whether it would have happened if the lessons from my accident had been learnt?

My colleagues in the Tiger Club, whatever their private opinions, were very forgiving – as indeed were my employers BEA. They might well have taken exception to losing six months of my services but BEA was a very paternalistic airline. I even had a sympathetic handwritten note from the chief executive, Henry Marking.

Any sensible person would have looked upon the accident as the end of any interest in sporting flying. Curiously enough, the club took the view that I would probably be a safer pilot after the experience. We had recently seen a superb demonstration by Belgian duo *Les Manchots* of formation aerobatics in Stampes which included 'mirror' flying where one aircraft flies immediately under its inverted partner. The Tiger Club wanted its own version and I found myself selected to be one of the pilots. Our initial practices were a little tentative using the club's single-seat Tigers. Several of our aerobatic experts such as Neil Williams, James

Gilbert and Bob Winter took the lead in the demanding inverted part of the mirror formation while I attempted to get as close as possible underneath.

Formation flying is difficult enough with low-powered aeroplanes but in attempting a mirror formation there is the further complication that the inverted aeroplane has a different angle of attack to the one right way up. It is therefore impossible to achieve a real 'mirror' image as the tails are always closer than the propellers. Furthermore, turbulence has a greater effect on slower aeroplanes, at times causing the safety gap to decrease alarmingly. Somehow the traditional British bank holiday weather seemed to ensure that turbulence was ever present.

By 1967, it was realised that that the superior aerobatic performance of the Stampe made it the obvious choice of aircraft and a pair were added to the act. A new pilot had joined the club in the shape of Pete Jarvis who had twice been aerobatic champion of the RAF's Central Flying School, making him the ideal leader.

Author in Stampe G-ASHS formatting on Pete Jarvis in a loop.© Brian Smith

The first time we practiced together I dropped back as usual to permit him to go inverted and had to marvel at the precision of his half roll. It was immediately obvious that this was a skilled aerobatic pilot in whom I could have complete confidence as a leader. We soon found we shared an interest in ancient anecdotes and dreadful puns. It helped initially that he had joined Comet fleet and we could arrange to have matching days off but we were split up when our double act nearly caused a captain to fail his annual line check for surrendering control to his crew.

Pete evolved a sequence which included formation stall turns, loops, mirror and opposed rolls-off-the-top which ended with us flying towards each other to execute flick rolls as we passed.

'You want me to do what!' Discussing the routine with Pete Jarvis, also in BEA and later captain with Air Europe.

The latter look very dramatic in a biplane so the sight of two aeroplanes seemingly out of control in close proximity to each other was a great crowd teaser. However, there is no doubt that the erosion of margins makes low level aerobatics extremely dangerous even in slow biplanes like the Stampe. The flick or snap roll is banned on some aerobatic aircraft because it is basically the dramatic precursor to a spin. Normally, the Stampe's double ailerons ensured immediate recovery to the wings level position but just occasionally they failed to arrest the incipient spin. That is what happened to our friend, British Aerobatic Champion Neil Williams, at a display at Biggin Hill. His life was saved on that occasion by the tendency of biplanes to absorb the shock of a crash as the wings collapse. Although the Stampe was reduced to a pyramid of wreckage, Neil escaped serious injury.

That said, at least eight of my contemporaries in the Tiger Club were killed in aircraft accidents. Strangely enough that attrition rate did little to curb the flow of young aviators eager to push their own personal margins. We survived on the black humour which had consoled WWII pilots facing infinitely greater danger. There was an inner chamber of the club known as 'The Black Cat Club'. The qualification for membership was to have survived the destruction of an aeroplane. Apart from Neil Williams and myself, its members included some well-known faces of the time such

116

as film actor Cliff Robertson and comedian Dick Emery. A proper constitution was drawn up full of quasi-legal jargon. Its clauses included one which suggested that, 'At the discretion of the committee, posthumous applications may be accepted!'

My next visit to Halfpenny Green was to prove that the airfield was something of a jinx as far as I was concerned. I was scheduled to lead the four-plane Turbulent team in a couple of displays, the second of which was to be at the scene of my near fatal experience. After the second take-off we flew in the usual loose gaggle until I gave the wing waggle non-radio signal for the other three to join up for a formation arrival. My Number 2 that day was another BEA colleague, Mike Channing. But as he slid smoothly into the slot alongside, a look of consternation crossed his face. Without radio he had no way of telling me what the problem was other than pointing below the wing, but from his fairly graphic hand signals I deduced that there was a problem with the left undercarriage leg.

There was no way of alerting Halfpenny Green to my plight but I waved the others away and elected to land along the left edge of the runway so that the sound wheel was on tarmac and the broken one was over the grass. Given the Turb's slow landing speed and coarse use of aileron, it was possible to keep the wing up to a point where it suffered little more than a scuff when it eventually made contact with the grass. It transpired that the port wheel attachment had fractured on departure from Booker and the wheel had been swinging gently in the breeze en route. The Turb was repaired and checked over and eventually flown back to Redhill. Strangely, I never felt any desperate need to chance my luck again at Halfpenny Green.

Comedian Dick Emery at Redhill. He survived a crash in his own Tiger Moth.

Romance

While at Renfrew I had met a lovely Scottish girl who seemed to be flashing green lights. At the time, however, I was suffering from broken heart syndrome due to the ignominy of being dropped by a previous fair lady. By the time my wounded ego had recovered sufficiently to be able to reciprocate her interest the new lady too had met somebody else. It seemed, however, that he was a bit of a playboy and treated her badly at times. On such occasions she would pick up the threads with me – usually when she suspected that I had met someone else.

In common with many of my generation I had expected to be married by twenty five but the on/off relationship with Helen dragged on through my late twenties. I was good friends with several other girls but none seemed to fit the nebulous ideal-woman image that an addiction to the cinema had planted in my head so I was reluctant to allow any relationship to become serious. One or two tried the 'I have met ***** and he wants to marry me' tactic. My response could only be to wish them well.

By the time I was in my thirties I had resigned myself to the fact that the ideal woman was not going to materialise and was happy to enjoy the companionship of some of our attractive cabin crew. Then, on one of our slip days in Athens we three pilots decided to book a trip from Piraeus round some of the nearby islands, undeterred by the fact that departure was at 8.00 am (6.00 am British time). Though this required reveille to be at 4.30 a.m. on our body clocks, the next morning found us sitting on board a little Greek tour ship, feeling faintly jet-lagged.

Contrary to any national stereotype, departure looked to be exactly on time. But, just as the Greek sailors were pulling the gangplank in, a taxi careered round the corner on two wheels and ground to a halt in a cloud of dust. From the taxi emerged a middle aged lady and a slim, brown-haired lass. The sailors took one look at the younger lady and pushed the gangplank out again.

As the two stepped aboard and joined our party the thunderbolt struck. For the first time in my life on meeting someone I thought to myself, 'I would like to marry that woman.'

It transpired that her name was Linda and that she was one of our Comet stewardesses on holiday with her mother. Though she greeted my captain as a friend and was happy to join in the chat as we toured the islands she showed not the slightest interest in me. The reason was revealed by my enquiries on return to London; she was already engaged to be married. It may sound quaintly old-fashioned but in my personal code wives and fiancées/girlfriends were off limits. So that was that.

However, a month or so later I was rostered for a Mediterranean trip which had a forty-eight hour slip in Malta. Who should be on the cabin team but Linda.

Left: Linda with Comet at Naples, 1965
Right: Linda in 1968 uniform.

As usual at the time, the whole crew went out for dinner and over a leisurely meal and a bit of dancing afterwards I discovered that not only had she been engaged for nearly six years but she was by no means certain that she was doing the right thing by getting married. The game was on!

Over the next day round the Phoenicia pool and another crew dinner it became obvious that there was indeed some mutual chemistry, though it progressed no further than a goodnight kiss. The lack of any such spark in Greece she explained later was due to her assumption that all pilots were married. As far as she was concerned, married men were off the radar. When we parted in Heathrow I gave her my phone number emphasising how very much I would like to meet her again but realising that the decision had to be left to her. To my absolute delight, she rang a few days later and our relationship took off.

Given the personal code aforementioned, I felt very guilty about hurting her fiancé. The only reason I can admit to it now is that he soon met someone else. They even got married before we did. Happily, they also became good friends of ours. As his wife pointed out, four people happy was better than two people potentially miserable.

Linda was indeed the girl of my dreams although it took me three years to persuade her to marry me. Her main objection was that she loved travelling and felt that children would interfere with that. Eventually, however, her priorities changed and when our two boys arrived she turned into the most doting mother that any child could wish for. We had thirty three years together before she was cruelly struck down by cancer. Looking back, I feel profoundly grateful to those early girl friends who had the good sense to abandon me for greener fields.

The rules had changed and Linda was allowed to continue to fly after we got married but, once it was clear we were to be parents, she was happy to hand in her wings. Approaching paternity also made me reconsider the wisdom of doing reckless things with aeroplanes close to the ground. My lucky escape with the Cosmic notwithstanding, there was no guarantee that my luck would hold in future bouts of low level aerobatics. Fortunately, the decision was made easier by the fact that the slow wheels of the seniority system had ground to the point where I would be offered a command course. Another challenging and exciting stage of my career was about to open up.

Vanguard

I t was in 1969, twelve years after joining BEA, that my name eventually rose sufficiently high in the first officer seniority list to be considered for command. Although this would involve moving to the bottom of the captain's seniority list and therefore switching aircraft, it was normal for potential candidates to be rostered for pre-command training on their current aircraft. Unfortunately for me, my mentor was to be the very training manager with whom I had the unfortunate disagreement over Comet crosswind landing technique.

Vanguard taxiing in at Renfrew in the '60s.

It rapidly became obvious that we had a major personality clash. In theory, the object of the exercise was for me to demonstrate that I could manage the flight. In practice, he would overrule decisions of mine on the grounds that they were not standard operating procedure – and then proceed to do something completely non-standard himself. Perhaps he considered me too much of a smart aleck for my own good but his blustering, bullying manner managed to destroy my self-confidence in less than a week. By the end of that time I could hardly even land the aeroplane I had been flying for over six years. Fortunately my long term track record was such that this loss of form was seen to be unexpected. The accepted remedy was a change of training captain and under more sympathetic supervision all became well again.

The normal progression for a new command would have been to the bottom of the captain's seniority list on Viscount 800s at one of the outstations. However, there had been quite an influx of new captains on the Viscount fleets the previous year. The Trident was now seen to be the future core aircraft of the fleet so the number of senior captains moving on plus normal retirements at 55 had created substantial vacancies on the Vanguard flight. So it was back again to the training centre for several weeks, pressing the eject button on my Comet technical knowledge and trying to upload replacement Vanguard facts.

Little remains in the memory banks of the ground course itself. The simulator was of similar vintage to that on the Comet with a limited range of movement and a visual system which depended on a camera with a moving map. Once again I found it difficult to accept that the feel of the controls and sensory feedback gave authentic representation of a real aeroplane. However, we were dealing with a different generation of trainers – men who saw that their duty was to teach rather than criticise.

As always, the eagerly anticipated part of the course was the base training which allowed us to get our hands on the real aeroplane. Stansted was still an under-utilised ghost airfield so was therefore the most convenient venue for most exercises.

The Vanguard was a fascinating aircraft. Overtaken by the jet age, it had never become popular with airlines or passengers. Compared to the Comet it was an ugly beast, prone to vibration and an unsynchronised beat from its four massive propellers. Yet it was a supremely efficient machine for transporting people or freight over short sectors. In BEA configuration it could carry 139 passengers and its cruise speed of 360 mph made it one of the fastest propeller aircraft ever built. This was particularly obvious in the descent when the flight manual permitted indicated speeds of over 300 knots (343 mph). Depending on height, these indicated speeds equated to true airspeeds of over 400 mph. More significantly, they were higher than those used by some of the jet competition. On short sectors, aircraft speed is less important than freedom from air traffic control congestion. The best illustration of this simple fact is that the published schedule time for Vanguard sectors such as Glasgow–London in the 70s was an hour and a quarter whereas the shiny jets of today have to be allocated one hour and twenty five minutes.

From the pilot's point of view the first impression was of the massive cockpit. It was possible to access the seats from the window side and each pilot had to have his own set of throttles. The interesting feature of the Vanguard's sprightly flight handling is that it was achieved without any of the hydraulically powered controls which are standard on jets. The controls were all manual but were assisted in their movement by a system of moving tabs. These worked so effectively that the aircraft handled extremely well at speed. The faster you went, the more delicate the response.

The spacious Vanguard cockpit. © *BA*

Rumour had it that Vickers test pilots had taken this apparently aerodynami-
cally challenged old lady to indicated speeds of over 400 knots (well above normal
jet speed) and in that range preferred its handling to that of the Vickers Valiant jet
bomber.

There was a downside of course. Any change of power or configuration involved
massive trim changes of both rudder and elevator. Selection of approach flap could
cause the unwary pilot to gain a couple of hundred feet. For landing, the airflow
from the props had an important effect on the elevators. Normal technique was to
make the initial flare with approach power on before closing the throttles. Once on
the ground the huge propellers went into a ground fine pitch setting which gave
excellent assistance to the brakes. If a strong headwind was present the deceleration
sensation was dramatic. In circumstances which required a short landing,
experienced pilots would close the throttles before the flare. Provided one was
prepared for the massive heave back on the elevator now required, the subsequent
landing run was impressively short.

But even in normal conditions the Vanguard had an excellent take-off and
landing performance. This undoubtedly contributed to the short block times
mentioned above in that the full length of the runway was rarely necessary. Take-
offs could be made from the first convenient intersection and the short landing run
at Heathrow on the northerly 28 Right was such that the turn off was usually very
close to the old BEA stands at Terminal 1.

Having got to grips with the normal handling we moved on to the required
training in engine failures on take-off and three-engine handling, including
overshoots from low level in the event of baulked landings. The most critical engine
in the event of failure on take-off was number four (the outside engine on the right-
hand side). We had already discovered in the simulator that a complete failure just
at the moment when committed to flight required an agricultural amount of left
rudder input to keep straight. Of course, on the aircraft itself there was no question
of engines being shut down for training purposes. Failure was simulated by the
training captain closing a throttle at the critical moment.

The exodus from Vanguards to Tridents had also included training captains
so some of our exercises were being conducted by trainers who were themselves
being trained under supervision. On the morning of my first introduction to engine
failure on take-off, the captain in the right-hand seat who was training me was in
turn under the supervision of his training manager sitting behind us. There was
a fresh crosswind from the right as we lined up on runway 23 at Stansted. As we
rotated, my trainer announced:

'Failure number four!'

All fired up in anticipation, I waded in with full left rudder to counter the expected swing. To my horror the aircraft moved left at such an alarming rate that we were over the grass in seconds before I reversed the rudder input and we climbed away on three. All the way round the circuit a sick sense of failure filled my being. I had messed up and this could mean the end of my aspirations to command and the ruination of my career. Meanwhile the trainer worked his way through the emergency and normal checklists. These required a final check on the simulated failure.

'Checking number one,' he said.

'Number one?' I expostulated. 'You said number four!'

Luckily the supervisor agreed. It would have been normal to fail number 4 but this was not done with a right-hand crosswind in case rudder control should prove insufficient. My apprentice trainer was so used to calling the number 4 failure that habit had taken over while his brain was involved in the mechanics of simulating the engine failure. On a swept wing jet aircraft, my error would probably have had disastrous consequences. In fact a Boeing 707 was lost at Prestwick during training in very similar circumstances. Fortunately the crew survived.

Our lucky escape taught a very useful lesson. On the early simulators without much in the way of feel of movement, there was a tendency to react by numbers to the information of a failure. In real life it is rare for an engine to fail instantly and it is much better for the pilot to react to his own sensation of swing and apply rudder proportionately. As my wise old colleague, Peter Harper, put it:

'Merely apply sufficient rudder to stop the scenery rotating about the cockpit!'

With its four powerful Rolls Royce Tyne engines, the Vanguard had another advantage for us to explore. In the event of a diversion away from base with engine failure, it was possible to ferry the aircraft home on the remaining three engines – although, obviously, without passengers. For this exercise we moved to the huge runway at Manston in Kent. In addition to being long it was also unusually wide so there was plenty of room for any unscheduled wanderings in our apprentice efforts. Fortunately the extra width was not required.

All in all the base training phase took nearly a week during which time I had amassed nearly thirty landings in various configurations of engines and flaps. With the vastly more sophisticated simulators of modern times, even new captains are lucky to get much more than a couple of hours and a handful of landings. Correct landing technique can be taught in the simulator and experienced pilots may simply go straight from there to flying under supervision with passengers.

Most of my own line training was done on the familiar domestic services to Manchester, Belfast, Edinburgh and Glasgow where the Vanguard was the standard workhorse. The final route check passed off without problems and at last I could have my uniform modified with that all-important fourth stripe. On 20 November 1969 I was rostered for airport standby to cover for any pilot who did not make his flight for any reason. But the night before, crew scheduling rang to allocate me to the London–Milan Linate morning service.

At long last, I operated on my first official BEA flight in command. The aircraft was Vanguard 951 G-APEC. Sadly it was lost nearly two years later when it plunged into the middle of Belgium after its pressure hull ruptured because of hidden corrosion. The subsequent escape of pressurised air into the tail section blew the surface off the horizontal stabiliser and caused a complete loss of control.

Vanguards had been the principal training aircraft for the early cadets from the training college at Hamble where they had completed a highly concentrated course expressly designed to prepare them for working in BEA and BOAC. Competition had been intense for the early places and the resulting graduates were of extremely high quality. So despite joining the airline with only about 200 hours experience they soon reached a high standard of instrument flying. This made them very useful team members in the monitored approach system. The area where their lack of experience was most apparent involved the more basic skills such as judging a visual approach to an airfield.

First trip in command: Vanguard hold capacity demonstrated by the volume of freight waiting to be loaded on Vanguard G-APEC at Milan Linate, 1969.

Strictly speaking, the Vanguard could have been flown by two pilots and indeed that was how it was operated by Air Canada. However, in the light of the massive training program of the sixties, BEA took the sensible decision to have a third man to monitor the others while dealing with the paperwork and getting the weather.

As a new captain, I found myself flying with some of the more experienced members of this generation who were very slick operators indeed. The drawback from their point of view was that new captains were not allowed to give away landings until they had accumulated a hundred hours of experience in command. Fortunately, our monitored approach system meant that co-pilots at least had plenty of practice in flying the approaches. Certainly the team operation made life easy for a new command, particularly as the route structure was a familiar one.

However, pilots are always assessing themselves by the challenges that they face. The more familiar the aeroplane became the more I sought to explore my limitations. I found myself studying the weather forecasts in the hope of finding extreme conditions to measure myself against. With increasing familiarity, I became impressed by the Vanguard's versatility and discovered more about her idiosyncrasies. As mentioned above, she could hold her own with the jet competition over short sectors. My best achieved Vanguard block time (i.e. startup to shutdown) between Belfast and London was 59 minutes. It was a time rarely bettered on jets. It apparently became necessary for a notice to be posted at London Air Traffic Control Centre:

'Please note that Vanguards descend at jet speeds!'

The most intriguing facet of Vanguard behaviour became obvious in crosswinds. I began to notice that it seemed easier to land the beast in crosswinds from the right – where the crosswind almost seemed to disappear. When the crosswind was from the left, on the other hand, there seemed to be an extra yaw at the last minute just when you thought the situation was nicely under control.

The reason became clear when you think about the standard Vanguard landing technique, whereby the aeroplane was flared for landing before the throttles were closed. The four massive propellers acted as massive gyroscopes and one of the curious features of a gyroscope is that any force applied to the spinning disc takes effect 90 degrees further round the plane of rotation. So the flaring of the aeroplane in applying a change in the vertical plane actually produced a force at the side tending to yaw the aeroplane to the left. With a right-hand crosswind the aircraft was applying its own correction; with the wind on the left there was an unexpected increase in crab angle at the last moment. This effect was accentuated by the closing of the throttles. It was one of many good reasons for closing throttles slowly.

European weather made sure that there were many opportunities to challenge a pilot's skill but, as always, there were also many amusing moments. My generation in their mid thirties were replacing senior captains in their late forties moving on to the Trident and others retiring at fifty five. As we approached the aeroplane down the jetty at Heathrow one day, one of the more mature chief stewardesses looked at the four shining new rings on my sleeve with a look of horror on her face:

'I don't mind policemen but this is ridiculous!'

To be fair I did look quite young for my age at the time.

We often had cause to be grateful for the quick wits of our cabin crew. The hijacking of aeroplanes to Cuba had become a feature of American aviation in the late 60s but the European scene was still largely unaffected. One day at Glasgow, the regular routine of our pre-start checklist for a flight to London was interrupted as the chief stewardess entered the cockpit.

'An American couple have just got on and the wife asked me what security precautions we are taking on this flight.'

'What did you tell them?' I cautiously enquired.

'Well I thought to myself, as far as I know, bugger-all – but what I said was, "Madam, I am not allowed to reveal that information!"'

Apparently they were very impressed.

Security

But, as we entered the 70s, dark clouds threatened the complacency of our secure domestic aviation world. The escalation of violence in Northern Ireland posed a potential threat to our crews night-stopping in Belfast and to the whole London–Belfast service (initially a Vanguard preserve but later a Trident operation).

The pilots' union, the British Airline Pilots' Association, was naturally concerned for the safety of its members. There had actually been a bomb at the crew hotel but, as management pointed out, it had not been intended as an attack on crew! BALPA found that of scant comfort and as one of the union officials I found myself involved in the front line of the debate. Our new hotel was located out in the country away from the daily violence of the Belfast streets. However, the last flight to Aldergrove arrived after midnight and entailed a trip by crew bus through some very dark and lonely lanes.

On one night stop I was supplied with a mobile radio to test whether I could alert our engineers in the event of an assault by the Provisionals on our transport. It was unclear to me what benefit this would bring in such an emergency but nevertheless the experiment had to be tried. It soon became clear that, while I could

Vanguard 951 G-APEB poses for the camera while at the Farnborough Air Show.

hear them, the engineers could not hear me at all. However, as I pointed out in my report, in the event of an attack on our engineers at Aldergrove, the crew might be amongst the first to learn about it.

Various procedures were put in place. Long before mass X-raying of luggage it was decided that passengers to Belfast would have to identify their bags before they were placed in the hold. One day as we arrived at the aircraft we noticed, standing proud among the line of suitcases, a cylindrical container over six feet tall painted a dull khaki colour.

'Looks like a bazooka,' I joked to my co-pilots.

Shortly afterwards, the dispatcher appeared. His mission was to co-ordinate all the services involved in getting the aeroplane away on time.

'Did you see the baggage?' he asked.

'What's that phallic object that looks like a bazooka case?' I responded.

'It's not a bazooka,' he confirmed. 'It's Blowpipe!'

Blowpipe was a shoulder-fired surface-to-air missile built by Shorts in Belfast. Although much more sophisticated than a bazooka, it never achieved much combat success.

'Who is the brave fellow who has this in his baggage?' I enquired.

'He's a little chap with an Irish accent who claims he works for Shorts. He says it isn't armed!'

'Has he anything at all in his possession that would encourage him in the belief that he can transport munitions of war on a passenger aeroplane?'

'He has a pass to Shorts' recreation ground!'

The story was so ridiculous that the passenger was almost certainly above board. Sadly, I left him behind anyway to learn the lesson that, in the atmosphere of the time, such baggage required a lot more security clearance than we had time to arrange.

As the security situation worsened, it was indeed rumoured that a bomb had been found on one of our aeroplanes, although not fully assembled. BALPA threatened to ban night-stopping in Belfast on the very day when it was my turn to operate the late evening service. As usual we had another return flight first, in this case to Edinburgh. When Operations wanted to know whether I intended to continue with the night-stop, I merely promised to decide on my return. As so often happened we would have a different cabin crew and it seemed only fair to make sure they were not unhappy about the situation. However, I did ask whether there were any high profile passengers on the Belfast flight who might be possible targets for the IRA. I was assured there were none.

Privately, my own view was that while the terrorists might threaten flights, they would not want to disrupt their own lines of communication by forcing BEA out of Northern Ireland. However, management had not been taking the issues seriously enough. On my return from Edinburgh I was amused to be confronted by an old friend, now an unhappy flight manager who had been dragged in by Operations in case I refused to go. There were some choice observations on my inadequacy as a captain in letting my cabin crew take my decisions for me.

As it happened, the forecast for Belfast was for limiting crosswinds and few eyebrows would have been raised if I had cancelled for that reason alone. The full load of passengers had already been advised that it might not be possible to land at Belfast because of wind strength. Satisfied with having set the cat among the pigeons, however, we caught our crew car to the aeroplane. At that time there was a boarding waiting area close to the jetty and as we climbed the steps from the tarmac we found our passengers already clustered at the top. My two first officers turned quite pale as we registered an imposing figure amongst them – no less than the IRA principal target of the time, the Reverend Ian Paisley!

'Good evening, Captain,' he boomed. 'What are our chances of getting in?'

'Fifty, fifty,' I estimated.

'You'll not take us South now, will you?'

I had to laugh at the thought of the headlines and repercussions of landing him in Dublin.

'No chance,' I reassured him.

Manchester or Liverpool would have to be our alternates. Fortunately neither was needed.

In a new initiative aimed at addressing security concerns, management produced another cunning plan reminiscent of the spy dramas of the time. It was decided that night-stopping crews should change out of uniform in the BEA office at the airport and, now disguised as civilians, take one of three pre-arranged taxis to the hotel. This we dutifully did one day and, having parked our bags, made our way across to the local pub for a much-needed refreshment. We entered to be greeted with a cheery,

'Good evening, Captain, what'll you have!'

He had never seen me before but, like off-duty servicemen, we stood out like the proverbial sore thumbs in that rural environment. We felt very sorry for the young men stationed in the province in a vain attempt to keep the peace. Often the guard posted at the bottom of the aircraft steps during the turn-round looked so little older than eighteen that the maternal instincts of the cabin crew were aroused and he was invited up to the galley for a cuppa.

Eventually, it was decided that night-stopping was too risky. There was a brief flirtation with positioning the empty aeroplane across to Glasgow and bringing it back the following morning for the early departure. That was clearly an expensive exercise so the next solution was to charter Loganair to take the crew across to Glasgow and back in the morning. Thankfully, sanity eventually prevailed and Northern Ireland was given the chance to develop its tourist trade and economic potential.

On a more cheerful note, visits to Dublin in the republic were often enhanced by the quick wit of the Aer Lingus staff who handled the turn-round. In order to save time, it was customary to send a signal from Heathrow before departure detailing the fuel required and maximum take-off weight for the return. Halfway across the Irish sea we would contact Aer Lingus operations in Dublin with any revisions to the figures. Despite this, a smiling dispatcher would come into the cockpit on arrival with a standard query:

'What would the figures be, Captain?'

When I responded one day with mild exasperation that we had already passed said figures twice, he replied without missing a beat.

'Ah you see, Captain, we have to have them in triplicate to avoid duplication!'

It was the same fellow who asked me one day:

'Do you know why there are so many silly jokes about the Irish?'

And after my request for enlightenment:

'It's so the English can understand them!'

In fact the worst and ongoing hazard to our quality of life was the ulcer-inducing industrial atmosphere of 70s Britain. London Heathrow was a particular hotspot where the trade unions ruled the land. Thanks to official and unofficial action it seemed that hardly a day went by without some dispute.

Fortunately the Vanguard had some useful features which were to prove invaluable in the dreadful industrial atmosphere of the time. With the new nose-in stands making it standard practice to start engines while aircraft were pushed back off the stand, tractor drivers had become essential members of the departure team and were just as prone to industrial action as anyone else. Fortunately the Vanguard was blessed with reversing propellers which enabled it to move backwards under its own steam; one of the novel pleasures of base training for budding captains was the opportunity to practice three-point turns. Before boarding aerobridges became the norm, sets of steps were also essential for passenger entry and exit. The Vanguard had its own extending steps which gave it independence in diversions as well as industrial action. Nevertheless, there was still a blessed feeling of relief when we moved away from the stand under our own power.

I did learn one useful lesson in passenger psychology, however. It is a matter of considerable resentment for many that they are so rarely informed regarding decisions about the operation.

We had reported for a routine Edinburgh flight, only to be told that it was the cleaners' turn to go slow. The passengers were being held within the terminal for an anticipated forty-five minute delay. I said we would go out to the aeroplane so that we at least would be ready in case the situation improved. We arrived at the stand to discover that the passengers had not been held but were in fact packing the little holding area on the jetty. Edinburgh passengers were not famous for their *joie-de-vivre* so I decided to go and have a word. After explaining the situation I had a sudden brainwave and offered them a choice.

'Ladies and gentlemen, you can wait here for forty-five minutes until your aircraft is cleaned to BEA standards or – if you are prepared to accept a dirty aeroplane – you can go now. Which do you prefer?'

'Go now!' came the instant chorus.

'Right, follow me,' I said and on to the aeroplane we trooped.

You have never seen a happier load of Edinburgh passengers. When they got off at the old Turnhouse terminal some even turned round to wave at the cockpit. There were no complaints about an untidy aeroplane – they had been consulted!

Early Vanguard visit to Frankfurt in 1961. (Photographed from a Comet which had actually entered service before it).

Lest it be thought that the above is just a piece of union-bashing, it is worth mentioning that, as an active member of our own pilot union, BALPA, I had been chair of the Comet flight local panel and served also on the main BEA Council. BALPA did not believe in waging a class war with our management. While we would fight hard for improved salary and conditions we also understood that commercial success for the airline was better for all employees. Progress in the industry was rapid and continuous so it helped that pilots as a group were only too ready to embrace new technology as it came along.

In the summer of 1970 a new bidding process was opened up. BEA had decided to start its own charter airline at Gatwick. Known as British Airtours, it would serve the holiday hotspots with Comets, now being displaced from frontline service by increasing numbers of Tridents. Keen to renew my love affair with the Comet as a captain, I applied and was duly accepted.

But then came a dilemma. My flight manager approached me with a promise of a training post if I remained on Vanguards. This was a tough call. If I took the Comet option there was a good chance there would eventually be training jobs in the new charter setup. The thought of playing a part in such a new venture was an exciting one. On the other hand, we had just become parents for the first time and the consequent move to better premises entailed a much larger mortgage. In the light of my new responsibilities, the bird in the hand seemed the safer option.

Late autumn saw me embarking on a course which involved being able to operate the Vanguard from either seat depending on whether captains or first officers were being trained. The importance of muscle memory in manual skills

133

was brought home to me when I returned to the right-hand (co-pilot's) seat. In BEA standard operation, pilots wore headsets all the time and all communication between the crew was on intercom. In moments of stress, when there was a lot of simultaneous information flowing into my headset from Air Traffic Control, weather broadcasts and crew, I found my right hand mysteriously rising up into the air. On analysing the phenomenon, I realised that my muscles had remembered that the communications box in the Comet had been in the roof of the cockpit. My right arm was reverting to its old role in attempting to reduce some of the auditory inputs. There had been no problem on my command course because the change to the left-hand seat had involved a completely new set of muscle movements to learn. It was the return to the right-hand seat where I had spent so many years that had re-awakened dormant automatic moves.

The next stage in the course was to be trained as an Instrument Rating examiner. In order to validate a commercial licence, every pilot has to undergo an annual refresher on his or her ability to handle the aircraft in various procedures by use of instruments alone. In the airlines these renewals are usually done in simulators by company examiners authorised to conduct tests by the Civil Aviation Authority (CAA).

In 1970, the CAA course which led to that authorisation was carried out initially on twin-engined De Havilland Doves. The Civil Aviation Flying Unit was based at Stansted which was still an oasis of calm compared to Heathrow and Gatwick. The CAA examiners carried out tests for the initial issue and renewal of flying licences and also used their aircraft to calibrate approach aids at licensed airports. This was where many a budding pilot had come in fear to be tested for the initial issue of the essential Instrument Rating. As mentioned earlier, my vintage were mightily relieved to have been tested on BEA's own Dakotas by company examiners.

First we were required to demonstrate that we were still capable of passing the test to the CAA's exacting standards. Fortunately the Dove was just as pleasant to handle as its big sister, the Heron, so the test was no more challenging than the annual renewals of the previous twelve years. Then we were introduced to all the criteria to be used in checking our colleagues. Eventually, we acted as examiners under supervision while the pilot introduced errors that would lead to failure in the test. This process was continued back at BEA's training block at Heston on our own Vanguard simulator until the supervising examiner was satisfied we would not completely betray the CAA standards.

In fact, like most new examiners, we were probably far too prone to nit-pick at first. With years of experience came a broader-brush approach. There was less emphasis on the initial error and much more on the manner of its recovery. Ultimately, the bottom line was whether one would happily let one's wife and family travel with the individual concerned. Fortunately BEA was able to recruit at such a level that few ever had any difficulty with the test. Simulators also made it very easy to repeat any item that had not been up to standard.

My generation, who had suffered under the Comet 'Gestapo', were determined that we would operate under the completely different philosophy we had seen on the junior Dakota and Viscount fleets. If pilots were trained before they were checked then the eventual outcome was to produce much better operators while wasting much less of company time. Pilots are usually highly motivated towards doing the job to the best of their abilities. They know only too well if they are having problems so the key training skill is diagnosis. As previously mentioned, there is little point in telling an experienced pilot that his/her standard is not good enough unless you can tell *why* things have gone wrong and, more importantly, what is needed for improvement

Training pilots are often selected on the basis of their own skills with some concession to seniority. There is no guarantee, however, that a smooth operator has any facility at teaching the less adept. In fact he may have difficulty in understanding why anyone else could have problems with something he finds so easy. There are even some sad individuals who are reluctant to pass on their inside knowledge lest their students surpass them.

Under the 'teach first' philosophy, the student who had problems arguably had a fuller course in that more elements of technique would have been analysed and explained along the way. However, even the best motivated trainer can occasionally have a personality clash with a student. Hence the thinking was that if someone hit a bad patch on a conversion the first recourse should be to change the training captain.

The training role was particularly important for BEA in the 60s and 70s given that the emphasis on recruitment had shifted from the RAF to the training colleges at Hamble and Oxford. The former took students direct from school while the latter dealt with University graduates. In both cases, they were joining on frontline aircraft with the minimum experience to qualify for commercial licences. That lack of experience was counterbalanced by the high quality of the applicant and the fact that their courses had been specifically tailored to the airline environment.

There was a notable difference between the products of the two colleges. It was obvious that Hamble students had been selected to a tight technical profile and that the disciplined approach of the college had constrained too much display of individuality. In the early stages it was as though they had been stamped out of a mould, albeit a high quality mould. The ex-university students from Oxford had had time to develop their personalities during their degree studies and were already characters in their own right. Job satisfaction for the trainer was immense because both lots were so highly motivated that they were a pleasure to teach. Many were to go on to reach high management and training positions within the airline.

Initial training was done in the simulator. Once students had demonstrated an acceptable standard of landing the machine at base they would fly with a training captain on commercial services until instructors were satisfied they had reached the standard of a competent crew member. In the end, however, we were merely providing another stage in a learning process which goes on throughout a pilot's career. There are recognised waypoints in that progression when the individual may fall prey to the temptation of believing that he or she is God's gift to aviation. Traditionally these have been held to occur at 100, 300, 1,000 or 3,000 hours. We reckoned that by 6,000 hours even great pilots realised that they were never going to know it all. The flying fickle finger of fate retained an unerring ability to spring a surprise. Even the best found that there was always something to learn.

The line training phase on passenger services often required a measure of fine judgement from the training captain. It was essential to allow the student as much freedom as possible to extend operating skills while being ready to interfere swiftly should something start to go wrong.

In particular, landings are much influenced by the different visual cues presented by individual airports. So a trainee who has demonstrated a consistent standard while practising repeated landings on the same runway at a training base may have problems when confronted by a succession of different ones. Slopes in the terrain before the runway or in the runway itself change the pilot's perception of the angle of approach. A wide runway can induce a flare too early while a narrow one can cause it to be too late.

One particular trainee had a tendency to initiate the landing flare too high – which can lead eventually to a hard arrival. After being debriefed on this issue he obviously resolved to correct the fault. At any rate, on his next attempt I realised at a height of about ten feet that he seemed to have no intention of flaring at all. I hurriedly grabbed the control column and pulled back – and the Vanguard's wheels kissed the ground in the smoothest landing of the week. As we turned off the runway, I cursed silently. My co-pilot was never going to believe that my intervention had saved us from a major impact. To my great relief our third pilot, the experienced first officer sitting behind, broke the silence with:

'Sometimes I wish I had a stick back here!'

The landing is perhaps the one part of the flight which carries the most weight in the passenger's assessment of the competence of a pilot. It has to be admitted that the outcome was not always so satisfactory in terms of passenger comfort as apprentice hands came to terms with landing in varying conditions. However, not even the most experienced aviator can guarantee a smooth arrival. Indeed in some circumstances, such as wet or slippery runways, pilots are actively encouraged to make a positive contact with the runway to ensure optimum and early braking. Given the ever-varying weather, the differing runway appearance and conditions, the changes in the weight and centre of gravity of the aeroplane, it is no surprise that landings can be as temperamental as golf swings. Yesterday you could do no wrong; today you can do no right.

This poses the question: what, if anything, should you say to the passengers if you have just made bone-jarring contact with terra firma?

My friend and colleague Bruce Cousins tried:

'Ladies and Gentlemen, sorry about the landing – which we would describe in technical terms as being bl**dy awful. I would like to tell you it was carried out by my first officer. Unfortunately, he won't let me!'

We did discover an interesting feature of passenger perception of the quality of landings. It varied with seating position – particularly in the longer aeroplanes. Sometimes a landing which seemed perfect in the cockpit would be complained about at the rear and vice versa. Passengers sitting over the main wheels may be over-influenced by a mechanical clatter as the gear makes contact and assume that there must have been hard impact. Although every pilot derives great job satisfaction from the perfect 'greaser', the quality of the approach and let-down to the airfield is considered to be the more important part of professional assessment.

Once a pilot had got used to the idiosyncrasies of the Vanguard, she was generally quite forgiving in the landing phase. But there was no better demonstration of her general robustness than an incident in September 1962 which could have so easily been a disaster. It was a filthy night at Edinburgh with a cloud base below 500 feet, heavy rain and a 20 knot crosswind. For the return flight to London on Vanguard G-APET, the first officer was the handling pilot. As they climbed away, there was suddenly a flood of white in the landing lights as they ran into a flock of seagulls. Number four engine failed immediately and there was a fire warning on number two which also failed. With air intakes choked with birds, the temperatures soared on the remaining two so that they should have been shut down as well. With the weather too poor for a two-engine approach at Edinburgh and Glasgow, Captain Denis Clifton's initial reaction was that they would have to divert to Prestwick. But with two engines completely failed and the two others throttled back to keep the temperatures from going off the clock, it rapidly became obvious that that there was no alternative but to attempt a return to Edinburgh for a manual let-down in the prevailing conditions with an aeroplane crippled with all sorts of electrical and hydraulic problems.

Every six months crews regularly practise such emergency procedures. However, for maximum training benefit to be extracted from the exercise, there is normally only one major failure at a time. Although sadistic examiners have been known to inflict multiple problems on a hapless crew, the result is usually to damage their confidence. On this occasion, it was no examiner's ego trip but rather a deadly serious situation. The cockpit was such a sea of red warning lights that it was difficult to decide which emergency checklist to action first.

That the eighty passengers and eight crew survived was thanks to a happy combination of circumstances. Firstly, the co-pilot flying, Ted Dunn, was a very competent operator. Secondly, the pilot in command was a training captain and therefore had an above average knowledge of the aircraft systems. In a Hollywood disaster movie the captain would have taken control and barked life-saving orders to his crew while performing unlikely miracles of handling. In this real-life scenario the captain knew he could trust his first officer to fly as safely as possible while he and third pilot Tony Gordon fought to establish priorities and restore sufficient electrics and hydraulics to lower flaps and undercarriage and provide the essential instruments and radio aids.

Despite all the failures and the problems of asymmetric power, Ted flew ET down the Instrument Landing System till the runway lights appeared at 350 feet, leaving his captain perfectly placed to take over for the landing. With the remaining engines failing rapidly they knew a go-around would not have been possible. When the runway was inspected, the bodies of a hundred and twenty five gulls were discovered in addition to those jamming the engine intakes. It was the ultimate justification of the monitored approach. The co-pilot's skill under pressure had freed the captain to manage a situation that with a different crew set-up might have been disastrous. Captain Clifton was awarded a Queen's Commendation and paid tribute to the calm and professional way his co-pilots had played their part.

Pilots practice regularly in the simulator for a myriad of possible emergencies which they hope will never happen. During my forty-odd years in aviation I have had occasional engine failures, but only one genuine engine fire. It was a routine flight to Gibraltar, a training sector for the co-pilot on his third week on the fleet. As usual on training flights, we were supported by a very experienced co-pilot in the third seat. At the time relations between Britain and Spain were at a low ebb over Gibraltar. As part of the campaign to regain control over the Rock, Franco had surrounded it with no-fly areas which made life as difficult as possible for pilots. When strong winds blow they give rise to severe turbulence in the lee of the Rock. Naturally such areas were traditionally avoided. In less diplomatically challenged times it had been customary to approach the westerly runway at an angle to avoid the worst trouble spots but the Spanish had carefully placed the no-fly areas to ensure that commercial flights had to fly through some of the worst of the turbulence.

On this occasion, wind strength was not a problem and the flight was proceeding smoothly as we approached Madrid. So smoothly in fact that I thought the moment opportune to take a comfort break. I had barely reached the cockpit door when the calm was disrupted by the shrill cry of the fire warning bell. No. 1 engine automatically feathered its propellor as it lost power. I called 'Fire Drill!' and leapt back into the seat. By the time I was ensconced the young man in the right-hand seat had shut the engine down and fired an extinguisher bottle. Fortunately the effect was immediate and the fire warning went out. When I looked round, my monitoring co-pilot had already picked up the technical log which records the aircraft's history of defect and was beginning to enter the parameters. It was a textbook exercise and I congratulated my trainee on his efficiency.

'That's all right,' he said. 'It's the second one I've had!'

It transpired that he had experienced an engine fire during the base training phase three weeks earlier. Two engine fires in three weeks while this one remained my only such experience in 45 years of flying! In a propellor-driven aeroplane the passengers were immediately made aware of our problem by the stationary propellor. I assured them we had dealt with the situation but would now have to divert to Madrid. Although the Vanguard could be ferried home empty on three engines, that would not be an option on Gibraltar's short 6,000 foot runway. A couple of minutes later the senior steward arrived in the cockpit.

'Captain,' he said, 'there is a gentleman down the back who is the editor of the main Gibraltar newspaper. He tells me that if you land in Spain he will be jailed.'

As a fierce advocate of Gibraltar's independence, he was certainly persona non grata with Franco. Rather than risk a diplomatic incident we decided to turn back to Paris which was blessed with BEA engineering cover and the luxury of long runways.

Despite his newly acquired expertise in Vanguard engine fire drills, I think my young co-pilot felt the fates were trying to tell him something and ultimately decided an aviation career was not necessarily the best option for him.

Vanguard GAPEU at Glasgow in the later colour scheme.

As Tridents added jet glamour to routes which had once been Vanguard preserves, a process started converting the prop liners to serve the less image-sensitive cargo market. Air freight makes Heathrow one of the most important cargo ports in the country - particularly in terms of high-value items. The Vanguard had always been able to carry significant amounts of freight in its under-floor holds. In the Merchantman modification a large loading door replaced the forward passenger entrance and the stripping of the inside furnishings revealed a cavernous interior which could accommodate standard loading pallets giving the old lady the ability to carry up to nineteen tons of freight.

For most pilots there was less job satisfaction in cargo operations but there were certainly some who felt the absence of passengers gave them a more relaxed life. While I was not one of that number, there were advantages from a training point of view in that trainees could be afforded more latitude without the risk of affecting passenger comfort. In emergency situations there was the further bonus that there was no need to worry about passenger morale. Returning one night to Heathrow from a Scandinavian freight jaunt, it became obvious that we had suffered a major hydraulic failure. While there were alternative means of extending wing flaps and landing gear we would have no brakes or nose wheel steering for taxiing. Given the length of Heathrow's southern runway and the massive deceleration effect of the huge propellers going into ground idle position, the brakes were not a problem insofar as the landing was concerned. So having come safely to a halt we followed the prescribed drill and asked the company to send the pre-ordered tug to tow us to our parking place.

Judge our dismay on being told said tug might take half an hour to arrive. Faced with the prospect of losing all kinds of popularity contests by blocking Runway 28 Left for half an hour, I decided to take advantage of some of the Vanguard's special tricks. The fact that the propellers could be put into reverse meant they could be used to stop the aeroplane while asymmetric thrust enabled us to turn. We left the runway and, emboldened by success, made our way cautiously to our correct stand, heaving a collective crew sigh of relief when the chocks were placed around the wheels.

As mentioned, the Vanguard could be taxied backwards using reverse thrust. The only danger was that brake applications had to be avoided going astern to avoid any risk of tipping the aircraft on its tail. That ignominy was an ever-present threat in freight operations as having too many pallets at the rear could prove too much for the centre of gravity. It was customary to fit a prop beneath the rear of the aircraft to avoid the problem but on at least one occasion the omission of this simple precaution had the inevitable embarrassing consequence.

Cargo was not always dull and boring. One colleague boarded the Merchantman for a night flight and in his pre-flight checks of the gloomy cabin noted that one pallet bore a large and impressive crate. As he attempted to read the tag on the nearest end of said crate he noticed his ankles getting warmer. Unable to read the tag he moved to a larger one on the other end of the crate. Strangely his ankles warmed up again. Puzzled by the phenomenon, he bent down to find the source of heat which seemed to be emanating from a grille lower down. In the darkness behind the grille he could see two round glowing circles about a foot apart. It suddenly dawned on him that he was looking between the eyes of one of the largest tigers he had ever seen. I have always loved the image of that heavy-breathing tiger gazing wistfully at a possible lunch outside.

Tridents

After three years on the Vanguard the opportunity arose for another move. It was no secret that BEA had made a major error in the initial Trident order. During one of the periodic economic downturns in the late 50s, the original deHavilland 121 concept had been reduced in size and its engines changed to less powerful Speys. DeHavilland was absorbed into Hawker Siddley in the early 60s so it was as the Hawker Siddley Trident 1c that the aeroplane became known in BEA. As it had been tailored to the *average* BEA sector, by definition it was implied that a full load would render the longer sectors beyond

Passengers boarding Trident 2 G-AVFN at Inverness.

Trident 3 G-AWYZ in flight. © *BA*

its range. This lack of flexibility torpedoed its chances of selling to other airlines with longer routes. Boeing shamelessly copied the three-engined concept with an aircraft much closer to the original De Havilland design. The resultant Boeing 727 went on to become one of the most successful jet airliners of its period. The Trident 2e was a much better version than its predecessor, the T1, with a modified wing and more powerful Spey engines which gained it the reputation of being the sports model of the fleet. Eventually there emerged a larger mark – the Trident 3b, capable of carrying 139 passengers. This was close to the size of the original deHavilland concept but it was far too late in the day to capture any export orders for Britain.

Commercial aircraft have a fundamental problem in that they are at their heaviest fuel-laden for take-off and therefore require enough power to give an acceptable runway performance. However, the size of engines required to deliver that power may prove uneconomic for the remainder of the cruise and descent. The Trident 3's typically British ingenious solution was to fit an auxiliary boost engine in the tail. Made of synthetic material, it produced an extraordinary 5,000 lbs of thrust with an additional weight of only 500 lbs (230 kilos). This 10 to 1 thrust ratio increased the maximum take-off weight to 71,650 kilograms and could be fired up for any performance-limited departure and shut down shortly after take-off once maximum power was no longer required.

In 1972 the Trident 3b was the new queen of the BEA fleet and therefore the target of most promotion dreams in the annual bid for vacancies. As promotion for line jobs was by seniority within the airline, it follows that Trident 1 & 2 fleet had a preponderance of senior pilots. Although some of these were indeed retiring, the subsequent vacancies would normally have been inaccessible to those of my generation's seniority. However, the Trident 3b was considered sufficiently different from her elder sisters to be a separate fleet. Those already happily ensconced on the older T1s and T2s were ruled out of the bidding process. Thus, unexpectedly, I found myself amongst a number of my junior contemporaries selected for the new fleet. Truth to tell, the situation may have been manipulated by the BEA managers to ensure that the crew establishment on the newest fleet was strengthened by an injection from the generation with the most previous jet experience.

Trident Conversion

The winter of 1972 saw the usual heavy Vanguard training programme continue for me right up to late on Christmas Eve. There was time to celebrate the day itself with a very pregnant Linda and the two-year-old Stuart before reporting back to Heathrow on Boxing Day for my last Vanguard trip, to Edinburgh and back.

Two days later I joined a bunch of my colleagues at BEA's Heston training centre for the Trident 3 ground course. Such courses are a regular rite of passage for pilots as they change types. You are required to press the eject button on most of the technical knowledge acquired (sometimes painfully) over the years on your previous aircraft and thereby make room for that technical knowhow deemed essential on the new machine. This was the last of the old-fashioned lecture-based courses I was to experience. In a time scale unbelievably drawn out by today's standards, we had five weeks to explore the mysteries of electrics, hydraulics, engines and instruments.

At the end, brains aching with theoretical detail, we had to face the dreaded hurdle of an exam set by the Air Registration Board. As previously reported, It was dreaded for two reasons:

a) It was set by engineers who tended to be more concerned with technical details considered somewhat esoteric by pilots who are mainly concerned with the *operation* of systems.

b) The high pass mark was required in individual sections as well as overall.

Fortunately, the instructors usually had a fair knowledge bank of previous questions which they were happy to share with us. That hurdle safely passed, it was onwards to learning the handling of cockpit procedures and the flying of the machine itself. As usual, most of the hard work was to be done in the simulator before entering an actual aeroplane.

Trident 3b G-AWYZ at Prestwick for base training.

In flying without visual reference the pilot is trained to rely entirely on the instruments and disregard any body cues which may mislead him/her into disorientation. But although the Trident 3b simulator was another step forward compared to the Vanguard version, it was still relatively primitive in conveying the feel of a real aeroplane. This particularly affected those pilots with a lot of experience in light aircraft or gliders who had learnt which senses they could rely on for perception of the forces acting on the aircraft. My own conversion was proceeding smoothly until it came to the obligatory practice of engine failures on take-off. A pilot must be able to demonstrate that, if an engine fails on one side, he can deal with the yaw and maintain an accurate climb-out profile to avoid any adjacent terrain in cloud. I found myself violently over-controlling to the extent that the supervising trainer would have had difficulty in signing the exercise off. This was not only mortifying for me as a trainer myself but puzzling for my partner in conversion.

Eventually, however, I reached the necessary standard in the exercise and a couple of days later we were on our way to Prestwick to fly the real aeroplane. From the beginning, I found the Trident 3b a delight to handle with none of the massive trim shifts with power and configuration changes that had been a feature of the Vanguard operation. In particular, the engine failure on take-off exercise was a non-event. What had gone wrong in the simulator, I pondered?

Realisation soon dawned. Pilots tend to carry physical habits from one aeroplane to another. On the Vanguard, the failure of an outside engine had required an agricultural input of rudder to keep straight. Fired up in anticipation of the failure, I had carried my instinctive reaction through to the simulator without realising that the close-coupled Trident engines required much less rudder for lateral stability. The danger of an uncorrected swing with engine failure is that it could rapidly lead to a wing drop and loss of control. In my rookie enthusiasm in the simulator, I had applied excessive opposite rudder too early and had actually swung *away* from the dead engine.

As mentioned in previous chapters, diagnosis is a key training skill and there is little point in telling an experienced pilot of an error unless you can tell him/her *why* it occurred. But my training captain had failed to spot that I was actually over-correcting and therefore swinging the wrong way. On the aircraft I could sense the yaw as the engine ran down and automatically apply just enough rudder to keep straight.

The Trident 3b cockpit with Hawker Siddeley's 'ramshorn' control column.

That was to be the last of the comprehensive base training sessions I was to enjoy in my career. Over four pleasant days living in the Caledonian Hotel in Ayr, my colleague and I carried out twenty-six take-offs and landings – each. Unheard-of extravagance nowadays as modern all-singing, all-dancing simulators are sufficiently sophisticated to the extent that experienced pilots in current practice can proceed directly from simulator to aeroplane full of passengers. The less experienced, or those requiring refresher training, may still be required to demonstrate their competence on an empty aeroplane but are usually restricted to one session with a minimum of three landings.

Trident Route Training

Armed with all the paperwork boxes duly ticked, I proudly presented my licence to the Board of Trade to have it endorsed for Trident 3b aircraft. I had booked a couple of weeks leave in the hope of being around to look after my wife before and after the arrival of our second child. But Peter Gordon stubbornly refused to put in an appearance till the night after I started my supervised training on the line with passengers. His late arrival presumably contributed to a birth weight of over ten pounds, which caused my slender wife considerable suffering over the thirteen-hour delivery and saw me banished from her side in the later stages. It became clear that she would not be allowed home for several days so my line training continued under some degree of stress.

At the time, the bizarre practice on the Trident fleet was for captains on conversion to do the initial handling sectors in the right-hand seat. From a training point of view this is counter-productive in that any improved familiarity with the cockpit is outweighed by the practising of the wrong muscle-memory skills. As mentioned earlier, these are an important part of the learning process. The practice owed much to the fact that some of the senior training captains of the time had spent little time as first officers and were not confident of their own ability to handle unusual situations from the right-hand seat. Some of them had been part of that 'Gestapo' I had encountered on Comets; men who had been given training posts on seniority rather than any talent for teaching or diagnosis. Fortunately the majority had a more enlightened attitude.

The members of the Trident family were beautiful flying machines. The Trident 1c was fast but the cutbacks in its size and power in the 50s had left it short of range and take-off performance. The design of its leading edge droop had contributed to the dreadful Staines accident of 1971. The Trident 2 was considered the sporting member of the tribe. It had a better wing with a proper leading edge slatted droop, better rate of climb and better range. As mentioned earlier, the Trident 3b was the heaviest, carried an extra 40 passengers and had been given the boost engine to improve that take-off performance which had seen the 1c cruelly satirised as the 'ground-gripper'! All Tridents had been designed from the outset to be capable of automatic approaches and automatic landings in fog. Part of the system was the use of automatic movement of the throttles to control speed on the approach.

Many of the new co-pilots on the fleet were graduates of the College of Air Training at Hamble with a total experience of just over 200 hours. The consequent large training programme had engendered a very conservative approach to standard operating procedures which those of us from more flexible fleets found somewhat frustrating. Standard practice was to use auto-throttle even on manual approaches. While that worked well in the still air associated with fog, it had several drawbacks in more unsettled conditions. Any speed fluctuations in turbulent air caused the power to hunt back and forth in a way which could be quite uncomfortable and even actually worrying for passengers seated near the engines at the rear. In manual flight, an inexperienced pilot could allow the attitude of the aircraft to vary which would further aggravate this hunting of the throttles. In fact the aeroplane was a very stable instrument platform, well suited to manual throttle operation

The Spey engines were incredibly noisy by today's standards. While that was all too obvious on take-off, I was puzzled to read that residents ten miles away in central London were complaining of aircraft noise on the approach, when you would expect operation to be on reduced power at 3,000 feet. The reason soon became clear. To give the automatic approach its best chance of trouble-free operation, approach flaps and undercarriage down were being selected in level flight *before* commencing descent on the glide-path. This additional drag in level flight required a large surge of power to maintain speed, which was not only noisy but wasteful of fuel. Nowadays, even with much quieter ducted-fan engines, there is a far greater emphasis on flying clean with flap and gear being selected much later on the glide-slope.

On the course, I dutifully complied with all the fussy procedures while making mental notes on how they might be simplified after escape from the heavy hand of training flight. But suddenly I developed a problem with the actual landing. Compared to its sisters, the Trident 3b had a natural tendency to skip slightly on touchdown but this had caused me no problem at all from the outset at Prestwick. One of the trainers who had done some of that early training was now supervising

Trident 3b at Munich.

my route work. He had been extremely complimentary about my handling at Prestwick but was now puzzled that my early skill seemed to have deserted me.

Once again there was a failure to diagnose the problem, but eventually I worked it out for myself. Under stress in the training scenario with the additional pressure of worrying about my wife and newborn child, I had reverted to an old muscle memory from the Vanguard. As mentioned, it was standard practice on the fleet to flare with power on so that propeller airflow over the tail gave better elevator control. I had been starting the flare in the Trident with the new-fangled auto-throttle still engaged and the consequent unexpected and unnecessary surge of power had altered the shape of the landing flare. It is obviously useful for a trainer to have some knowledge of the converting pilot's previous aeroplane so as to be alert for transferred bad habits.

That problem solved, I passed my final check, although the check captain criticised my descent into Heathrow at 320 knots (about 365 mph) as being 'a bit faster than you are used to'. Discretion being the better part of valour it seemed diplomatic not to mention that that sort of descent speed had been common on Vanguards – to say nothing of the T33's maximum in a dive of 505 knots (about 580 mph). We were given post-training questionnaires for any comments we might care to make. Mine was to the effect that the course was very pleasant – provided one did not actually need any training or help.

So began ten enjoyable years of Trident operation which eventually encompassed all three marks.

Despite much mockery visited on the early models for a lack of take-off performance, Tridents were De Havilland's dreadful experience with the first Comets ensured that subsequent British commercial jets were built like the proverbial brick outhouse. Tridents seemed to provide a more comfortable ride in turbulence than their larger and longer American successors which were more prone to fuselage flexing.

From a pilot's point of view they were very stable instrument flying platforms. In particular Hawker Siddeley had provided superb flying surfaces. The swept wing had been designed for the high speed of the Trident 1c. The slower speeds of the approach necessitated changing the wing profile to a curve by having a movable droop for the leading edge in addition to the usual flaps on the trailing edge. The high-mounted tailplane was an all-moving device and the ailerons remained effective down to stall speeds. Whereas any configuration or power change on Vanguards required considerable trim changes in elevator and rudder control, the Trident was a remarkably stable beast. When trimmed to a speed in the descent, it seemed content to fly at that speed regardless of droop, flap or gear configuration changes.

Although the alteration of the wing profile by leading edge and trailing edge devices permitted slower flight on the approach, these speeds were still high compared to Trident contemporaries. Landing close to 150 mph on short runways demanded much of the wheel brake system but the Trident had another trick up its sleeve. Most passengers are familiar with the roar of engines being placed in reverse thrust after touchdown to reduce the load on the braking system. This technique was taken a stage further in that reverse thrust could be selected on the outboard engines in flight. Not only did this make available some exceedingly dramatic rates of descent in the event of Air Traffic Control failing to provide timely clearance but, by making the selection just before touchdown, any undesirable runway-eating float was eliminated. With the aeroplane flared for landing there was also a component of the thrust now acting vertically to ensure good contact with the surface on a wet or slippery runway. It has to be said, however, that it was prudent to warn the passengers beforehand for a sudden roar of power before touchdown could otherwise be downright alarming.

But even with this assistance, on landing there could be considerable heat build-up in the eight main wheel brakes. In a short-haul, quick-turnaround operation this could reduce the efficiency of the brakes should there be any need to abort the subsequent take-off. So the bogies were fitted with brake fans to assist in the cooling process. In the event of a known fan failure, the ground engineers would arrange for an air bottle to produce the required cooling effect. As there were no brake temperature gauges in the cockpit, the somewhat unscientific test of adequate cooling was the ability to hold one's fingers on the brakes for a few seconds!

We landed at Dusseldorf one torrid summer's day with little headwind and a temperature of 36° C. One of the brake fans was unserviceable and the ground crew were slow at getting an air bottle into operation. By the time they did so, the temperature in the offending brake system was well above the tolerance of the most asbestos-skinned fingers. We had no option but to announce a delay to departure. Having always believed in keeping passengers in the loop, I explained in layman›s language the need to ensure the brake temperature was within limits before take-off.

The chief steward arrived in the cockpit shortly afterwards.

'There›s a lady down the back,' he reported, 'complaining bitterly about British Airways and our record of delays. She claims to have a very important deadline in London.'

Never one to shirk facing the paying customers, I volunteered to go and explain the situation to her again. The lady was not for listening, however.

'BA are always late,' she informed me. 'I write for the ******** and I have a very important deadline for my editor in London.'

As I attempted to explain the situation further, a passenger got up from a few rows in front and intervened,

'Don't listen to this,' he said. 'She's being going on like this since she got to the airport. She gave the check-in staff a helluva time. As far as I'm concerned – and I'm sure I speak for the rest of the passengers – we are happy to wait until, in your judgement, it is safe for the aircraft to proceed. And if this woman gives you any more trouble, my name is ******* ******* and I write for the Sunday Times!'

Collapse of stout party – her ace trumped!

On most flights you could expect to have at least one passenger to be completely unreasonable, perhaps for personal stresses such as the very common fear of flying. If the captain is seen to be dealing with the issue in a sympathetic and sensible manner, the majority of the other passengers will normally take his or her side. Where the complainant was seen to be unreasonable, it was not unknown for others to intervene – as in the above example – along the lines of, 'Why don't you tell him [and it was usually a him] to f*** off!'

Delay before departure boarding presents a special case. Modern airports make it difficult but, where possible, it was always worthwhile for the captain to explain the real reasons for a delay to the passengers at the gate. Otherwise failures in communication would leave the ground staff dependent on general blanket excuses such as 'operational reasons'.

If passengers were told the authentic reason by someone they tended to trust and (more importantly) were told what was being done about it, they were more likely to board the aircraft without taking their frustrations out on the cabin crew. The result was, generally, a much happier flight for both passengers and cabin crew.

In August 1977 it was discovered during routine engineering checks that cracks were developing in the wings of Trident 3s. This caused aircraft to be grounded while a fix was found which involved an extra patch on the underside of the wing. As usual, the British media were quick to exploit any opportunity to attack a national airline. When we boarded our aircraft for an afternoon flight we found that the *Evening Standard* being passed out to the passengers had banner front page headlines about Trident wing cracks. Fearing the effect on those nervous passengers who are reported to constitute 20% of the average load, I felt it necessary to say something.

'Ladies and Gentlemen, you will have read in your paper that the wings might fall off this aircraft at any moment. Let me just say that if that indeed were true neither I nor any other member of the crew would be on board.'

The pleasure taken in attacking our own products and institutions seems to be a particularly British phenomenon. Other countries seem to take their patriotic responsibilities more seriously.

Earlier on that very year a Dan Air cargo Boeing 707 had crashed in Africa when part of the tailplane failed due to metal fatigue cracks. As it belonged to a minor airline and only the crew were killed it barely merited a mention in the UK press.

Rare sight of a Trident 3b (G-AWZV) at Berlin Templehof.

In fact the Tridents were stoutly built, as were most British aeroplanes after the Comet 1 disasters. When they were phased out in the 80s, the firm that had the contract for their break-up found that massive amounts of oxy-acetylene were needed for the task. In the end they resorted to using cranes to pick aircraft up by the wingtip and dropping them from a height to break the wings!

The Trident 3b soon became the workhorse of the BEA fleet capable of carrying its 139 passengers to any airport in the European mainland network, although the UK domestic services were the bread and butter backbone of the workload. BEA had introduced the very popular 'shuttle' concept whereby passengers did not have to book but were guaranteed a seat provided they turned up at least ten minutes before scheduled departure. In order to fulfil that guarantee it was necessary to have spare Trident 1s or BAC 111s with crews on standby. In theory, the back-up might despatch with a solitary passenger; in any event, its load would normally be less than that of the scheduled aircraft so its rate of climb would usually be better. This led to some less-than-mature gamesmanship when the back-up crew would make every effort to overtake the scheduled service and land at the destination first.

The shuttle concept was particularly popular with the business community at the mercy of over-running meeting times, even if it meant that catering had to be sacrificed for the taking of fares on board. The frontline service aircraft could depart as soon as it was full, leaving the back-up to collect the stragglers. This operational flexibility also meant that passengers turning up early for their flight might find themselves ushered onto an earlier service, thereby sometimes avoiding the need for a back-up at busy times. Although the boast was that a back-up could be provided for even one passenger, every effort was made to avoid such waste. If necessary, passengers could be offered financial incentives to wait an hour or so for the next departure. However, this practical approach to commuter flying could not have survived the subsequent world-wide expansion of the security industry.

As well as the domestic services, mainland Europe was our oyster. A normal day's work would be three or four flights. A four-sector day would involve two return trips from Heathrow, e.g. London–Glasgow return followed by London–Copenhagen return. As the schedules included late flights into and early flights out of most European cities, night stops were required. Typically, an early domestic return service might be followed by an evening stop in places such as Rome, Geneva, Paris or Frankfurt. While this afforded crews opportunities for pleasant outings in interesting cities, the corollary was a crack-of-dawn wake-up call for the early departure, followed by another return excursion out of Heathrow. In places like Athens (two hours ahead of the UK), a seemingly reasonable 6.30 a.m. alarm call was actually 4.30 a.m. on our body clocks.

Particularly in summer, the routine European agenda was occasionally enlivened by visits to more exotic destinations such as Tangier, Agadir or Tunis and charter flights brought experience of other off-the-beaten-track airports. It was a particular privilege to fly sick pilgrims into Lourdes. On the other hand, charters for orchestras such as the Philharmonia demonstrated that professional musicians can pose a severe threat to bar stocks on board.

It is the unusual airports that are the most interesting to the pilot. At the major European cities, the main danger was that familiarity and excellent approach aids could breed complacency. Demanding airfields like Gibraltar did ensure that crews were on maximum alert.

In 1974 one of the most interesting charters was a night flight to Krakov, then firmly behind the Iron Curtain. We were familiar with the major cities such as Moscow, Budapest and Warsaw but BEA had never operated into Krakow. The airport was to be kept open through the night especially for us. On my first arrival there we found that our turnaround time more than doubled from our usual 45 minutes to two hours. While this was largely due to the meticulous scrutiny of our passengers by immigration and customs officials, there was only one lady to clean the aircraft and the baggage loaders were not too enthusiastic about having to work in the middle of the night. The Trident was a noisy beast and we had arrived at 2.00 am local time, presumably waking up most of the surrounding neighbourhood. Just as they all resettled to their slumbers we created even more disturbance by taking off at 4.00 am.

On my next visit, I found that distributing a few miniature whiskies to the cleaning lady and the loaders considerably enhanced their enthusiasm levels. I also took the opportunity to pay my respects to the air traffic controller in the tower. Amongst other things I apologised for our noise footprint, then a subject of considerable agitation in Britain.

'Don't you get any complaints about the noise?' I naively enquired.

'Of course not!'

His tone was that of a man who could not imagine an ordinary person would dare raise a complaint against the system. It was an interesting insight into life behind that infamous ferrous curtain. The skies were lightening as we lined up for take-off and I just could not resist torturing my co-pilots with a dreadful pun.

'You realise that we are watching the actual Krakov dawn?'

All-weather Operations

A t the time I first joined BEA in 1958, the most important winter weather problem was fog or, more particularly, smog. Smog was a vile mixture of fog and the sulphurous coal smoke of the time. In high pressure cold and near-calm conditions in winter it could set in for a week or more and visibility could drop to less than a hundred yards.

As mentioned in the chapter on BEA Renfrew, Glasgow was particularly prone to these traditional pea-soupers. Visibility could deteriorate to the point where it was impossible to see across the street. Driving had to be at snail's pace, trying to maintain visual contact with the pavement edge. The old tramcars, being unaffected by navigational problems, were god-sent guides for the motorist.

For the pedestrian, things were even worse. Apart from the dangers of crossing the street, breathing in this muck aggravated the respiratory problems all too common at the time. Blowing one's nose left a sooty deposit on the handkerchief.

In an era of less sophisticated instruments and navigation aids, clearly such weather had a major impact on aviation. For BEA our problems at Glasgow were nothing compared to those in London. This was the main base and hub of all operations so any fog delays there had massive repercussions for the whole network. Thus the airline had taken an early decision to seek more sophisticated autopilots with a view to allowing automatic landings. Although the monitored approach team operation on Vanguards had permitted approaches in visibilities as low as 350 metres for manual landings, the Trident was intended from the outset to be capable of automatic landing in much worse conditions.

The process of working up to approval was a long and tedious one, which had contributed to the pedantic procedures I had thought so restrictive on conversion. It had also involved a triplication of the autopilot controls so that one rogue error could not exert undue influence. Gradually the permitted approach limits in terms of height and visibility became lower and lower. Eventually we were allowed to descend to 14 feet before seeking visual reference for an automatic landing. While this would almost certainly guarantee visual contact, we had to demonstrate that the aeroplane could overshoot safely from that height. Naturally this had to be practised in clear conditions at our training bases such as Prestwick and Shannon. The go-arounds were scrutinised very carefully by air traffic controllers for if the wheels actually touched it counted as a landing and thus incurred a higher charge!

More interesting was the decision as to the lowest visibility in which an approach could be permitted. Theoretically there need be no limit as the ability to descend to 14 feet should guarantee visual reference. As a member of the BALPA technical committee at the time I was privy to the discussions when this vital issue was debated. In fact the final decision was in the hands of the Heathrow firemen. Their representatives argued that their colleagues would be unable to find an aircraft in visibilities of less than 75 metres and so that became the lowest permitted for an approach.

Through continual practice of procedures the landing soon became a non-event. The difficult part was finding the arrival stand in the murk. At Heathrow that was made easier by a system of lead-in green lights which could be followed on taxi-ways together with considerable help from ground movement radar in the tower. Charts were developed of the taxiways with helpful headings so that the co-pilot could monitor the captain's path.

However, landing in itself is not sufficient to maintain schedules unless further take-offs are possible. Tridents were fitted with indicators on the instrument panel which could be linked to the Instrument Landing System on the runway so that any deviation from centre line caused a horizontal rolling barber-pole effect which compelled an instinctive correction. With this and the excellent runway lighting essential for approved runways, take-offs also were permitted in 75 metres visibility.

Thanks to the high quality of the young pilots emerging from Hamble Air Training college and continual practice, the much-mocked BEA monitored approach system triumphantly came good in fog. The team operation became very slick indeed and at home base, Heathrow, the controllers came to expect that Tridents were infinitely flexible when it came to accepting any changes. We were happy to co-operate, knowing the favour might be returned when we requested shortcuts.

A classic example occurred one dark and gloomy night when the visibility was only 150 metres on both easterly runways. In the old days that would have been a definite diversion case. We had just locked onto the Instrument Landing System (ILS) for the usual Runway 10 Left (now 09 Left due to the subsequent changes in magnetic variation) when the controller asked somewhat apologetically if we could possibly accept a switch to the southern 10 Right in order to allow fire engines to cross 10L.

'No problem,' I replied.

'Roger, turn onto a heading of 140 degrees, call established 10 Right.'

There was no need to say anything to my two experienced colleagues. As the co-pilot turned onto the new heading, the third man leaned over and changed the ILS receivers to the new frequency. We checked the identification signals, reviewed the changed go-around procedure and in a trice were established on a successful approach to the other runway.It has to be said, however, that the traditional British sense of fair play ensured that the UK was usually one of those European countries where the national airline could not expect to be shown favouritism. The situation was often different in the Mediterranean countries where use of the local language could sometimes allow the national airline to achieve priority. Germany was not normally one of those countries but in the all-too-common periods of European air traffic control disruption, paranoia can break out.

Legend has it that on one occasion a British Airways flight called for start-up clearance at Munich and was given a two-hour delay. Shortly afterwards, Lufthansa called and was given immediate clearance. Justifiably miffed, the BA captain complained about this clear favouritism but the Lufthansa captain deftly laid to rest the myth about his country's lack of a sense of humour.

'Ah, you see, Speedbird, we were up very early this morning. We already have our towels on the runway.'

The Merger

The great aviation issue of the 70s was the proposed merger of the UK's nationalised airlines, BOAC and BEA plus the smaller Cambrian and Northeast airlines, to form British Airways. While an amalgamation clearly made sense in terms of integration of services and reduction in duplication, the airlines had very different operating philosophies.

Many pilots are tribal by nature, tending to assume that the procedures they are expert in must be the only true religion. In truth to tell, my later experience was to convince me that pilots were much the same in most major airlines. While it was true that the job security of the UK national airlines ensured they could have the pick of available talent, crews were to some extent featherbedded by comprehensive support systems throughout their networks which did little to encourage thinking outside the cockpit. In charter airlines operating away from base to smaller airports with foreign handling agents, pilots had to be much more involved in the overall operation.

Tribal loyalties were widespread in both main national airlines. BOAC crews carried the British flag round the world, enjoying a lifestyle which tended to encourage a belief that they were the *creme de la creme*. There was a certain condescension in the way some of their cohorts dismissed short-haul pilots as mere 'puddle-jumpers'. It seemed that a conservative approach to new ideas was endemic in the airline and that this had been reinforced by the sort of checking-rather-than-training attitude that had made my life a misery on joining Comets.

Life in BEA was more work-a-day than glamorous but the continuous practice afforded by multi-sector daily patterns ensured a high level of expertise across the fleets. The airline had never been afraid to experiment with new methods and there was much more emphasis on a crew working as a team. As more and more of the old school retired, training flight was now dominated by those that believed that teaching came before checking.

BEA's monitored approach operation in limiting weather conditions had led to a standard operation in which the captain did the take-off and landing but handed over to the co-pilot for the en-route and approach phase until there was sufficient visual reference to land. Roles were reversed when it was the co-pilot's leg. This posed a particular problem for the big sister line where it was still fashionable for the handling pilot to operate as a one-man-band while the other pilot looked on admiringly.

In the early days, training captains in both airlines had been recruited more on the basis of their own competence and seniority than any evidence of a talent for teaching. In an attempt to improve matters, courses were set up on instructional techniques. As part of this programme it was arranged for training captains to attend a practical course at the Hamble college where the majority of new pilots were being trained. Ostensibly, this was to provide continuity in linking the cadets' airline aircraft introduction to their Hamble course on Piper Cherokees and Beech Barons. In practice it was an opportunity for us to learn some teaching tips from experienced *ab initio* Hamble instructors while the light aircraft handling gave us an insight into the cadet experience.

As part of the course we all took the aptitude tests which formed part of the assessment of potential BA pilots. Some of us were by no means convinced that we would have cleared this hurdle. In particular I put it to the invigilator that these tests were geared to the selection of those of scientific bent. His deadpan reply was rather chilling for an arts graduate.

'We have not found arts to be a positive factor in selection!'

There was also an opportunity to mix with our long haul training colleagues and a few of those contacts confirmed the gulf in philosophy. One was actually heard to say, 'I wouldn't presume to tell another pilot how to fly!' That this was not an isolated view was confirmed by the first short haul co-pilots to move on to long haul aircraft. While some received the sort of early sympathetic assistance they had been accustomed to, others spoke of a complete dearth of guidance on the new aircraft and its associated unfamiliar route structure.

For BALPA the problem was the integration of the two different pilot lists. Promotion in both airlines was by seniority subject to progress. Any relative loss of position on the combined list might make a huge difference to, for example, time to command. When the various railway companies were amalgamated into British Rail after the war it was said that more than twenty years later drivers were still getting on and off trains at the boundaries of LNER or LMS operations. It took a lot of blood, sweat and tears at BALPA national councils and the annual conference but, thanks to some far-seeing souls on both sides, the dyed-in-the-wool sectarians were vanquished and the necessary compromises were eventually agreed.

As both airlines had recruited from Hamble, it was relatively easy to agree a seniority date for these pilots in line with their order of graduation from the college. For the more senior, mainly captains, it was agreed that the problems were so intractable that the easiest course was to ban any cross-bidding at all.

Officially British Airways was formed on 31st March 1974. In 1981 the Conservative government instructed the Board to prepare for privatisation but it was February 1987 before the airline was floated (very successfully) on the Stock Exchange. As nationalised companies, both main previous constituents had been bloated by layers of middle managers so after the merger the combined staff numbers peaked at around 60,000. In the years after flotation this number was pruned by over 20,000 in middle management, apparently without any adverse effect on operations.

Amongst pilots it still took many years for some to abandon previous loyalties but the problem slowly disappeared as the old guard retired. While for me personally it was a matter of some regret that I would never get a go at Concorde, my next short-haul aircraft was to prove a much more marketable qualification when the time came to leave British Airways.

Boeing 757

$\mathcal{I}$n the early 80s there was much excitement in the air. British Airways was looking for the next replacement for the main short-haul fleet. Airbus and Boeing were making representations about the Airbus 310 and the Boeing 757 respectively. For those pro-Europe, the Airbus seemed the obvious choice, if only to demonstrate some commitment to the Common Market. Not only would it

Brand new G-BIKC Edinburgh Castle *gleaming in the early morning sun at Boeing Field, 2 February 1983. Captain Norman Hutchings, Boeing pilot Ed Hoit and the author.*

160

bring wide body spaciousness to short haul but it also had the advantage of being able to use the same cargo and luggage containers as BA's long-haul fleet.

The B757 on the other hand was to be a completely new aircraft with untried Rolls Royce RB211 engines. Its narrow one-aisle body would require dedicated cargo containers while the massive under-wing RB211 engines required that passenger doors be at wide-body aircraft height. It shared a cockpit layout with its larger sister, the wide-body B767, so that pilots could operate them both on a single licence.

On the face of it the decision was a no-brainer. But that was before Boeing's formidable sales team got into the act. This was to be the first Boeing aircraft offered from the start with British engines. As a launch customer, together with Eastern in the States, BA was made an offer on price that could not be refused. There would also be an obvious benefit for Rolls Royce.

When a demonstrator visited the Engineering Base while appearing at the Farnborough Air Display, we pilots pored over it like children in a toy shop. The cockpit was clearly a descendant of the legendary B707 and B727 but the instrumentation was an early example of the 'glass' cockpit revolution wherein versatile cathode ray tubes replaced countless conventional instruments. The star feature was that the old-fashioned compass was now incorporated into a visual display of the route. Inertial navigation would greatly reduce the dependence on ground-based beacons and VORs. In addition, the computer capability would enable us to construct vertical paths in the sky. To my great delight, I was chosen to join the training team which would introduce the new aeroplane to BA – particularly as the training course involved was at Boeing's base in Seattle.

Anticipation mounted as the B757 simulator was delivered to BA's training centre at Cranebank. This was in a different league to the simulators for older aircraft. A huge box mounted on swaying hydraulic legs, its freedom of motion gave sensory inputs much closer to the feel of a real aeroplane while its computer-generated visual screens could replicate a huge range of weather situations. Our appetites whetted by the opportunity to play with this new toy, we embarked enthusiastically on the task of training our replacement Trident instructors. Four days before Christmas I operated my last Trident flight: a quick evening LHR–Paris Orly return.

Excitement built as we discussed arrangements for the 757 course which was due to start on 3 January 1983 at the Boeing base in Seattle. It was decided that our group accommodation would be in a block of self-catered flats with two of us per flat. As it would be necessary to leave between Christmas and New Year the company agreed that families could join us for New Year's Eve before serious work commenced.

BA had no direct Seattle flight at the time so it was to San Francisco we departed the morning after Boxing Day. After a short night-stop at the airport Holiday Inn we were on our way to Seattle. As we walked along the jetty towards arrivals I noted a twin-engined B737 across the tarmac with what appeared to be a similar but much smaller executive jet parked next to it. There followed a swift double-take as I realised that the 'executive' jet was in fact a B737 and its much larger cousin was the new wide-bodied B767, already in commercial service.

This was the long range aeroplane which was to prove that twin-engine operation across the Atlantic was a practical and safe proposition. More relevant to us was the exciting spectacle of a more slender plan view in the sky as B757s made approaches to Boeing Field. The unusually large dimensions for a narrow-bodied aircraft explain why it soon acquired the nickname of 'stick insect'. We had a course party to celebrate the New Year and had a couple of days to relax with family and get over jet lag. 1 January 1983 proved to be a red-letter day as Eastern Airways operated the first commercial B757 flight from Atlanta to Tampa.

Serious work for us began with Ground School at Boeing Field which was also to be the handover airfield for our new aircraft. This section of a conversion course had changed considerably in the ten years since my Trident equivalent. Boeing had the practical philosophy that there was little point in teaching pilots obscure technical material unless it was relevant to the operation in the cockpit. Maximum use was made of computers, cockpit procedure trainers and simulators to familiarise the pilot with his physical working environment. Regular tests checked that vital operating information was being absorbed.

Unfortunately the Boeing philosophy had yet to reach the hallowed halls of the UK Civil Aviation Authority. After a mere two weeks it was time for the most dreaded hurdle on any conversion course – the technical exam set by the engineers of the Air Registration Board. As touched on in earlier pages, these tests were notorious for setting questions more relevant to aircraft engineers than pilots.

However, on previous courses there was always sufficient folklore accumulated from those who had gone before to prepare for some of the more obscure questions. As this was the first entry of the B757 onto the British register we had no such friendly buffer. Two days later I learnt to my horror that for the first time in my flying career I had failed an exam, as had about a third of my colleagues. The result was humiliation for the British Airways contingent and mystification for Boeing instructors who had seen us regularly accrue marks of over 90% in their exams. At a subsequent post mortem I posed one of the questions to Boeing's Chief Ground Instructor:

'OK – on which stage of the RB211 engine is the oil pump?'

His reply was a clear statement of the Boeing philosophy that there was little point in burdening pilots with technical information on matters over which they had no control in the flight deck,

a) I don't know!

b) Who the s**t cares?

c) What could you as the pilot do about it even if you knew?'

It is difficult for the lay reader to understand the effect this setback had on the morale of those who had experienced it. As senior training captains in British Airways we were at the peak of our profession and representing our airline in a foreign country. Although we all subsequently passed a re-test, the humiliation was deeply felt and its after-effects took many years to pass.

The ARB stuck stubbornly to their guns and such questions remained in the paper. After our experience, however, the cat had been released from the bag and another body of folklore built up to save future generations from our damaging experience.

For the next two weeks we put our new found knowledge to practical use in the full flight simulator which, as noted in the previous chapter, replicated more faithfully than ever before the instrument indications and feel of a real aircraft.

The B757 flight deck – its six cathode ray tubes marking the transition from conventional instruments to 'glass' cockpits.

The B757 cockpit was a transition in design. As mentioned earlier, it was still an obvious descendant of the legendary B707, B727 family except that two cathode ray tubes in front of each pilot had replaced basic flying instruments of yore. Another two in the centre console replaced multiple instruments relating to engine and system parameters. Either side of the throttle quadrant were the computer screens and keyboards which were the pilot interface with the aeroplane's sophisticated navigation system in both horizontal and vertical planes.

This was the greatest innovation for pilots. Instead of navigating along airways by tuning beacons and VORs and following needles which pointed towards them, an entire route could be inserted into the autopilot's memory and then displayed on the lower of the two pilot CRTs in diagrammatic form. The weather radar could be fed into the same display so that there was instant appreciation of the effect any weather phenomena might have on the route ahead. Radar could also show terrain so coastlines helped to confirm position. The actual pattern of runway departure and arrival procedures could be displayed. With en route winds entered into the computer's brain, expected times of arrival at en route points and destinations were instantly available and were usually accurate to within a minute or so.

From the beginning, the B757 had been planned to follow the Trident's pioneering work in being capable of automatic landing in fog. The autopilot could be used to lock on to approved Instrument Landing Systems and would eventually be cleared to land in visibilities as low as 75 metres. We had been used to that on the Trident but this computer had a further useful trick in its electronic brain. Vertical profiles could be constructed even at runways lacking sophisticated aids so as to give the preferred standard 3 degree glide path to touchdown. There was still a requirement to observe the limits appropriate to whichever old-fashioned aid was available but the virtual glide path ensured a smooth and controlled descent to decision height.

The artificial horizon was still a central instrument in the upper display in front of each pilot. It was fitted with a flight director in a pretty shade of magenta. This consisted of a vertical and horizontal line which followed the same laws as the autopilot. In other words, provided the manual pilot kept them nicely crossed in the centre of the instrument then any demands selected with regard to lateral or vertical flight were being complied with. The only danger was that over-concentration on the 'magenta line' as it came to be known, could lead the inexperienced to be less aware of the basic attitude of the aircraft.

Most of the flight engineering panel, which would have required a third crew member on previous large aircraft, had now been replaced by the two cathode ray tubes on the central console. Not only could they display all the usual engine instruments but also alert the pilots to any malfunction of the aircraft systems.

The simulator proved to be an excellent introduction to the novel features of the aeroplane and heightened anticipation of the big day when we could actually get our hands on the real machine. For Pat Farrell and me that day proved to be 2 February 1983 and the aeroplane was G-BIKC, newly handed over to BA. At that time, BA still named their aeroplanes and the B757 fleet bore the names of British castles. The fact that KC was christened *Edinburgh Castle* seemed an auspicious start for a couple of Scots and Pat very kindly let me have first go.

As our brand new shiny ship soared off the north westerly runway at Boeing Field it soon became obvious that its handling was well balanced and even more pleasant than the simulator had predicted. After exploring the edges of the flight envelope at altitude, we crossed the Cascade Mountains to the much quieter airfield at Moses Lake. The massive runways remaining from its military heyday as a Strategic Air Command B52 bomber base in the 60s were ideal for the take-off and landing circuit training which is an essential part of any conversion course. Its 4,100 metre main runway had made it a suitable diversion field for the Space Shuttle.

To save time, training landings are usually of the 'touch-and-go' variety. On a normal touchdown the air brakes on the wings go to maximum deflection (or 'lift-dump' position). As the name suggests, this kills lift on the wings and wheel braking is applied. In training landings brakes are not used but instead the instructor resets flaps to the take-off position, selects lift dump 'in' and applies take-off power while the trainee sets off on another circuit.

Trainers have to be able to handle the aeroplane from either seat but once we were content with our own normal and single-engined operation we made instructor Ed Hoit a very happy man. His usual role was watching others fly but now he was appointed as the 'student' so that we could practise resetting the controls on the runway.

With the obligatory paperwork completed we had time for a few celebratory drinks at the Blue Max. Next day, we boarded a flight to San Francisco to catch the BA 747 home and, for me, a reunion with Linda and the boys. After the usual visit to the CAA to have my licence endorsed with the new type it was back to work on the BA simulators training the next course of pilots.

The first British B757 commercial flight was to Belfast on 9 January 1983 but, with only two aeroplanes available, it was the 17th before my own line flying initiation could be fitted into our tight training programme. For practical engineering reasons early flights were confined to the domestic sectors but it was very pleasant to be

*The author on base training duties with **G-BIKD** Caernarvon Castle at Stansted, which in 1983 was virtually deserted by today's standards. **G-BIKT** Carisbrooke Castle in the newer livery at Aberdeen in 1986.*

showing off our pride and joy to Edinburgh, Glasgow and Belfast. Although I had had my own private misgivings as to the wisdom of operating a busy programme with just two aeroplanes of new design and engines, the 757 came up trumps. Yes, we had a few teething problems with false warnings from the monitoring computers. Although the aeroplane made more use of computers than anything we had previously flown, its early computing power was considerably less than that of a modern smart phone. Changes of plan en route could lead to the somewhat discomfiting screen message 'Stand By'. But, by and large, the introduction to scheduled service was remarkably successful. By the end of March two more aeroplanes had arrived and as the fleet gradually increased so our route network broadened out to the usual busy European destinations.

The Rolls Royce RB211 fitted to early B757s was a remarkable example of the rate of development in aircraft engines. Its 37500 lbs of thrust was modest by today's standards but each engine developed more power than all three Speys on the Trident – even when the boost engine on the Trident 3 was factored in. Both engines together had two and a half times the power of a Trident and yet not only used less fuel but were also considerably quieter in operation. Development of the engine had been traumatic for Rolls Royce but its acceptance by major American airlines led to a significant breakthrough into world markets and the start of a dynasty of engines which are now found all around the globe.

Twin-engine aircraft will always have a more impressive performance on normal climb-out because the regulations demand that any terrain clearance required on departure be achieved even with an engine failure at that critical point on the runway when the flight is committed to continue. Therefore a twin has to be able to comply with any climb-out restrictions on 50% of normal thrust while four-engined bigger brothers would have 75% still available. It follows that on a normal take-off the twin has a surfeit of power.

No surprise then that ex-Trident pilots in particular revelled in the sparkling performance of the B757. At Heathrow, it was common for departing aircraft to be held down by London departure control to 6,000 feet until they had cleared the area of the four holding beacons which feed the airport. On first contact with departure control it became standard to promise, 'Can give you high rate of climb.' That this was no idle boast was demonstrated on one easterly departure where there was a requirement to be above 3,000 feet within 10 miles. On being released from the 6,000 feet restriction we passed over that gate with 7,000 feet to spare. Apart from saving fuel by allowing aircraft to reach their most efficient operating level sooner, there was also the bonus of reducing noise over metropolitan London.

The B757 soon became the versatile workhorse of the British Airways short-haul fleet, as comfortable on long sectors to the eastern Mediterranean as it was on the short dashes to Manchester, Brussels and Paris. Admittedly, the shorter sectors did pose a challenge to our cabin crew in an era when food and drinks on board were still free. While flight times were the same as those on the Trident, a full aircraft carried another fifty passengers in its 189 seats. In particular, early evening domestic services were full of tired business people desperate for their first dram or G&T.

In order to reduce any dithering about choice of drinks, it was useful to make an extra announcement before take-off on the evening Heathrow–Manchester.

'Ladies and gentlemen, the flight time tonight is 35 minutes - which gives the cabin crew a working time of about 25 minutes. We have bet them they cannot get round you all with the drinks trolley before we put the seat belts sign on at Manchester.'

Minds were concentrated!

As the fleet expanded the training programme was continuous. An interesting feature was the arrival of the first senior co-pilots from the long-haul fleets who had volunteered for captain vacancies on short-haul. Most of them had enjoyed the long-haul lifestyle but, having been there and done that, were at a stage of their lives where they preferred to spend more time with family free from jet-lag. Their arrival highlighted the difference of training philosophy between the old BOAC and BEA touched on in the previous chapter.

As discussed earlier, BEA took the view that pilots should be taught before they were checked. By the time a pilot was senior enough for command he or she had accumulated a thick file from all the various checks along the way. If these had been consistently satisfactory the general anticipation was that the command course was more of a seat conversion exercise than a real hurdle. Trainers initially gave every assistance and then gradually reduced their support to the level of dim-witted novices.

In other airlines command candidates were put under pressure from day one, ostensibly for them to prove they had the mettle to be captains. My first two ex-long-haul command candidates in the simulator were very pleasant gentlemen. But, as I embarked on my usual comprehensive brief for the first detail, I realised they had already swotted up religiously on everything I was telling them. For one who had never believed in tribal differences between airlines, it was gratifying when it was generally accepted that we were on their side.

As the fleet grew, Boeing made some production line modifications to the original aircraft. In particular there had been the odd problem in other airlines with tail scrapes on landing. It was decided that the lightness of control which had so delighted us in our first experiences might be a contributory factor. In particular, the elevator forces were stiffened up.

Eventually it became necessary to fly aircraft back to Seattle for various modifications, thus allowing some of us to experience the long-haul end of B757 flexibility. We could not have flown Heathrow–Seattle with a normal passenger load but it was no problem with an empty aeroplane. Against the prevailing westerlies it took ten hours and fifteen minutes to cover the 4,800 miles. The return was, as usual, quicker at nine hours and twenty minutes.

One particular flight stands out from December 1983. There had been a couple of days of the strong southerly crosswinds which can be a feature of the Jersey weather so that a considerable passenger backlog had built up. It was decided to send the 189 seat B757 for the first time and I had the pleasure of landing at the airfield where I had learnt to fly the Dakota. At the time, John Nettles was filming his very successful series *Bergerac* in Jersey and he came into the cockpit to thank us for the rescue act.

Moving on: Air 2000

*I*n 1986, BA was gearing up to become a private company and, as part of the necessary changes in the interests of efficiency, early retirement packages were on offer. In those days BA pilots had a compulsory retirement age of 55. An early pension was available together with a handsome capital sum. Much as I enjoyed the B757 operation, a few problems had arisen to blight the job satisfaction. In particular there was another personality clash with one of my bosses. More importantly, a bit of me was always keen to try something different. So, with a mere 21 months to go, the thought of a capital safety net for the first time in my life seemed too good a bargain to turn down. My colleague Pete Harper took the same decision.

On 29 December 1986, I operated a morning return flight to Milan Linate followed by the short dash to Amsterdam. Linda joined me for this, my last night-stop with BA. After the return from Amsterdam the next morning there was still an Oslo return to complete as my last BA flight. My co-pilot was happy to be given the afternoon off as he was replaced by my old friend Bruce Cousins who was also a training captain on the fleet. He signed my logbook to the effect that I had passed!

That evening we brought in the New Year in some style with a party at home which kept us out of our beds till nearly five in the morning.

So it was that the beginning of 1987 found me unemployed for the first time in my adult life. Some thought had to be given as to whether it was worth my while to seek further employment. It was true the Thatcher government had reduced the top rate of tax from the punitive rate of 83% under Labour to a mere 60%. Even so,

Air 2000 B757 on take-off from Heraklion, Crete.

by the time National Insurance and pension contributions were taken into account, less than a third of any new salary would end up in my account. Was it worth sacrificing my new life of leisure? I had been running the first regular classical music programme on Gaelic Radio. Was there a possibility of developing that interest? In the meantime, interesting opportunities were opening up on the aviation front. In particular, there was talk of a new charter airline to be based in Manchester, operating brand new B757s. I wrote to the flight operations director suggesting that what he really needed was a couple of ex-BA 757 instructors.

There was little love in the charter sector for the perceived prima donnas of BA. However, Captain Neil Burrows was familiar with the short-haul emphasis on teaching and agreed to hire Pete Harper and myself on a three-month contract to help get his embryo airline off the ground.

In the 1980s, some UK charter airlines operated at a fairly basic level. This new airline Air 2000 was set up by Owners Abroad Ltd, a company which already had a track record of improving that image. The Air 2000 management team was a strong one. Managing director Errol Cossey had made a success of Air Europe, commercial manager was the workaholic Angus Kinnear and the charismatic flight operations director, Neil Burrows, was to prove one of the best bosses I have ever worked for. In charge of the vital job of training the cabin attendants who would be the main interface with the travelling public was Customer Services Director Glenda Lamont who had come from Gulf Air. Thus the new airline's service model was to include hot meals, Buck's Fizz for breakfast and such legacy airline touches as hot towels after meals.

In the cut-throat economics of the modern era wherein free food and drink are but distant memories even on major short-haul carriers, hot meals might seem

171

like mindless extravagance. Errol Cossey explained that hot meals were easier to provide than the previous charter staples of salads and sandwiches. The latter had to be freshly prepared and, given the early departures of most charter flights, would have involved expensive out-of-hours payments to catering staff. Hot meals could be prepared in advance and frozen so as to be reheated in the on-board ovens. Instead of relying on foreign caterers, food for the return flight could be carried in the aircraft holds. The brand new B757s would seat 228 customers – nearly 40 more than the BA ones on scheduled services. They were resplendent in white, red and gold – surely one of the finest colour schemes ever devised for the type.

Pete and I set up a Flight Training Consultancy registered for VAT to mitigate the tax implications. We met up with Neil Burrows on 19 February 1987 and nine days later found ourselves in a hotel room in Seattle to meet the pilots who were to be the start-up crews for the new airline. It was more than a little disconcerting to find that many of them were ex-Laker Airways. Freddy Laker was the charismatic entrepreneur who had set up his airline in the 70s to provide cheap 'no-frills' trans-Atlantic flights. Initially very successful at tapping a market which would not normally contemplate long-haul travel, the airline had eventually become a victim of the recession of the early 80s. Its demise had been hastened when a group of the legacy trans-Atlantic airlines dropped their prices to compete. While this group included most of the big names such as Pan Am, TWA and the main European carriers, there was no doubt that Laker staff particularly resented the part played by British Airways. It was not surprising if our new companions might be deeply suspicious of our usefulness to their conversion course.

The course itself was to be conducted by Boeing instructors. Our previous Seattle experience in 1983 had shown us that the simulator exercises were regarded more as competency checks than training exercises. It was our intention to brief each crew in detail as to what they might expect, observe the detail and de-brief on any problems with advice on how they might be rectified. In normal BA short-haul simulator training we would also have given advice throughout the early sessions before final checks. As mentioned frequently in previous chapters, we had found that an emphasis on teaching initially before final checking produced much better long-term results. The Boeing instructors regarded that as 'coaching' which was not allowed on conversion. However, all was well in the end. Gradually even the ex-Laker guys realised we had something useful to offer.

The American attitude to bureaucracy was refreshingly different from that prevailing in the UK. Pete and I thought it would be useful to have an American licence in case we wanted to do any private flying in the States. We called at the Federal

Aviation Agency office at the airport to enquire into the possibilities. Within half an hour we had been issued with a temporary commercial licence with the promise of a formal version within a few weeks. If we wanted the Instrument Rating necessary for flying in cloud, it was only necessary to complete a short questionnaire. The process would have been infinitely more complex in the UK, or indeed in the EU.

Having completed the simulator training part of the conversion course, for me it was a passenger trip back to Manchester to be ready for the arrival of the brand new G-OOOA. Crewed by Neil Burrows and Pete, it arrived precisely on schedule despite the fact that the inertial navigation system had been playing up en route. It was welcomed to Manchester in some style with the Halle Orchestra playing for a reception on the pier. The guard of honour was provided by cabin crew whose black and white checked jackets reflected the fashion of the time.

The first priority was getting the company's new pilots on line as soon as possible. The next few days were spent visiting various airfields where light traffic permitted the circuit training necessary to give each pilot the obligatory refresher minimum of three landings.

In the old days Prestwick would have led the list but rising landing charges there meant that it was often worthwhile to journey further afield to Brest and Nantes in France and Shannon in Ireland.

The necessary circuits are usually conducted at 1500 feet and despite the quietness of the Rolls Royce RB211 engines compared to the previous generation, complaints about noise at Nantes reduced its usefulness to us. However, at Prestwick I discovered a novel method of simultaneously reducing the time between take-off and landing while minimising the noise nuisance for the local community. As many airlines have realised through the years, the long main runway at Prestwick 13/31 is ideal for this type of training. Orientated south east/north west it gives a final approach to 13 over the sea. From a noise point of view, ideal for landing; not so good for take-off. However, as the wind was a light crosswind I suggested to the tower that we do our take-offs on 31, perform a 'dumbbell' procedure turn over the water to reverse heading and return to land on 13. They were only too happy to acquiesce.

Then the big day of the airline's inaugural flight arrived on 11 April 1987. The flight was the 0610 Manchester–Malaga return and it was a privilege to be supervising two captains, Alan Blake and Keith Castle, who were destined for key positions in the airline. Sue Devereaux was the No. 1 in charge of the cabin crew. The flight time of two and three quarter hours each way gave them a reasonable timeframe to put their training into practice and, despite the obvious pressure of the unfamiliar, their enthusiasm for the new service was a delight to see.

G-OOOA at Malaga for Air 2000's first commercial flight. Captain Alan Blake second from right. (Captain Keith Castle in the cockpit doing the turn round checks). The cabin crew in the original black and white checked jackets with No. 1, Sue Devereaux, fourth from left. The author in the middle.

In BEA/BA, Pete and I had often regretted the 60s split between pilots and cabin crew rosters which had sometimes seen us fly with three different cabin crews in the same day. There was no doubt in my mind that *esprit de corps* on the aircraft suffered as a result. Fortunately this was not a problem in Air 2000 where all on board were part of the same team. In fact the quality of the product inspired remarkable levels of enthusiasm among all who worked for the airline. Thus the three months of line training passed all too quickly as the airline branched out to favourite holiday spots in the Mediterranean and the Canaries.

The main operational flaw, however, was the usual summer problem of Air Traffic controllers in France and Spain using the peak summer season to take industrial action. In Europe, congestion on the airways requires each departure to have an available slot aloft before permission is given to start engines for take-off. Clearly the problem is much exacerbated if traffic flow is being artificially restricted. If only one country was involved it was usually possible to find an acceptable detour, even at the cost of massive delays. However, I arrived for a June morning flight to Faro to find that both French and Spanish controllers were going slow and there were huge delays projected before start-up permission would be given. It does not require much knowledge of geography to understand that an airways routing to Portugal without overflying France and Spain would not only add considerably to the journey time but would create further problems for the busy German airways.

But our shiny new ship was equipped with the triple Inertial Navigation Systems which were a requirement for operating in Atlantic airspace. I rang up Shanwick control in Ireland and enquired whether we could route over the sea to the 15° West meridian outwith French and Spanish airspace before turning east under Portuguese control. Not only did they have no problem with that but we were given immediate clearance to start -- much to the amazement of some of the flights belonging to more senior airlines at Manchester.

That was nothing compared to the situation at Faro. We arrived to find competitors' aeroplanes parked all over the place; some with huge delays and others actually cancelling flight plans so as to night-stop as crew ran out of duty time. Our passengers were called on time and we felt unbearably smug as, once again, we were given immediate clearance to start. Despite the slightly longer route length the round trip was only ten minutes longer than usual. Commercial Director Angus Kinnear was famed for his fairly low opinion of pilots as a group but even he cracked a wintry smile of approval. We used the route again over the next few days for Faro and Tenerife. For the latter it made even more sense and it has become a standard routing to the Canaries from the north of England and Scotland.

Canada 3000

*I*t was indeed a Tenerife flight that concluded the contract for me on 24 June. The next day I made my way back home to Surrey for my second retirement in six months. While I saw much more of the family and the garden benefited from increased attention, I was also still running a classical music programme in Gaelic for Radio nan Gaidheal in Glasgow. In addition, I was given the opportunity to do some reporting for the current affairs programme *Prosbaig* on Gaelic TV. As always, I was fascinated by a different technology. However, it was by then the twilight of the old-time news teams complete with director, cameraman, sound man, lighting man, assistant cameraman and the director's PA. As apprentice reporter, I was definitely lowest on the pecking order. The cameras still used film packs which only lasted ten minutes but the operators were experts in their craft.

The writing was on the wall. Although the cameramen spoke glowingly of the superiority of film in the creation of mood, the difference in quality between Outside Broadcast and studio pictures was all too glaringly obvious. Nowadays, a single reporter with the latest portable digital camera can produce stunning quality footage while more and more use is made of material shot on smart phones.

Accustomed as I was to an industry where training was fundamental and continuous, my main difficulty was that I was expected to pick up the necessary skills without much in the way of briefing. Initially I was not even aware of the ten-minute film limitation and tried my director's patience by taking too long to get to the nub of an interview. In the end, the programme itself came to the end of its life – taking with it my nascent TV career.

Then in June there came a phone call from Neil Burrows. Air 2000 had come up with a novel way to cope with the winter dip in holidays which followed the summer season peaks. In Canada the position was almost the exact reverse. As we had discovered thirty years before, Canadians flocked to the Florida and Caribbean sun in the winter but were happy to enjoy their own climate in summer. The solution seemed blindingly obvious; set up a Canadian sister airline which could use Air 2000's aeroplanes in the winter and return the favour in the European summer. Would Pete and I be interested in another training contract for the set up of this new venture?

This sounded like fun, not least for the opportunity to spend some more time in a country of which I had so many happy memories from the 50s. So it was back to the simulator to refresh the obligatory checks which dominate a pilot's life before renewing our acquaintance with the aeroplane in September. Having had several prolonged lay-offs from flying in my life, I find it quite interesting that the first few landings after such a break were invariably some of the best ever. As some find with golf swings, constant practice does not always produce the best results, perhaps because an element of complacency creeps in.

The first task was to supervise the training for the Canadian crews. Although there were perfectly serviceable B757 simulators available in Luton, it turned out that it would be cheaper for this to be done in Singapore. Not only did Singapore Airlines have cheaper simulator rates but as part of the package they would fly crews out to Singapore in the comfort of their business class. Untrammelled by any notions of political correctness, Singapore Airlines had built their cabin service reputation around their extremely attractive young cabin crew. But they were not just pretty faces. The excellence of their training was evident in such details as remembering the passenger's name. Of course other airlines used this ego-enhancing trick by associating names with seat numbers. What was impressive on SIA was that the attendant at the exit door was still able to remember names on wishing passengers goodbye.

The final deal clincher was that there had just been an explosion of top-class hotel building in Singapore and bargain rates were available that rendered Luton's exotic charms non-competitive. As we settled into the luxury of what was then the Westinn Plaza next to Raffles we manfully strove to conceal any nostalgia for the UK facilities.

The Canadians proved to be a varied and pleasant bunch, many of them ex-RCAF. Interestingly, one of them was blind in one eye. This was apparently acceptable to the Canadian authority although something of a surprise to those of us who had always assumed that 3D vision must be essential to the hawk-eyed pilot. However John proved to be perfectly capable of landing the aeroplane. Dusty Thompson was to be the chief pilot and a little ritual evolved of talking shop round a pitcher of Tiger beer across the road in Raffles. That is until the evening Dusty announced that he had found a restaurant with free food. Naturally it was necessary to check out this improbable claim. Sure enough, a Chinese meal washed down with Tiger could be had at Fatty's for the cost of a similar quantity of beer alone in Raffles.

Further culinary delights ensued as we explored the hawker stalls of Newton Cross. The memory is still warm of the freshest prawns I have ever tasted; stir-fried straight from the tank in a street cafe. Even in the luxury hotels, Asian cooking of authentic style could be had for very reasonable prices. For those nostalgic for home customs the high-speed lifts in the adjacent Stamford shot smoothly up over 90 floors in 60 seconds to their rotating restaurant. Afternoon tea was a special treat as the views of the city slowly changed.

Those views of course were still in the process of being revolutionised as Singapore left the shabby chic of the past far behind. The charming Chinese lady in reception briefed me on the new underground which was indeed a revelation. Stations were bright and airy, the modern feel softened by greenery. Immaculate trains operated in air-conditioned tunnels, sealed off by glass panels. Long before London got round to the idea, doors opened in the glass wall to correspond with the doors of the arriving train, thereby preserving the air conditioning while eliminating suicide opportunities.

My report back to my adviser was enthusiastic, if slightly exaggerated.

'It was so clean you could have eaten lunch off the floor!'

A look of horror crossed her elegant features.

'Ah, not allowed to eat food on underground!'

Under Lee Kwan Yew, Singapore was well on the way to becoming the Tiger economy it is today. Much to the displeasure of the left, rigid discipline had eliminated litter and chewing gum from the streets. I remember a lady writing in the Australian press about how she had asked her taxi driver from the airport what sort of country she was entering.

'Very bad country – no freedom.'

'So why is there so little complaint?' she enquired.

'Everybody got job, everybody got house, everybody got money in bank; nobody want to complain!'

At the end of the simulator sessions, we were booked to make our way to Toronto with Air Canada. The contrast with Singapore Airlines was stark. As Canada is the ultimate in political correctness, there could be no question of cabin attendants being chosen for youth and ability to charm the tired business passenger. Plum international routes were crewed through selection by seniority. On our flight via Bombay the youngest member of the cabin crew was thirty-five and she was there only because she was a last minute substitute from airport standby.

Now selection by seniority is all very well if the extra years in the job translate into excellent customer service. That was not to be our experience. The meal out of Singapore was airline international standard chicken. The meal out of Bombay was – you've guessed it – more chicken. All cabin announcements were made in both English and French. Whether in the interests of parity or not, they were done equally badly in both languages.

To be fair to Air Canada, similar seniority systems operated in the once-great American airlines Pan Am and TWA. It is not too fanciful to speculate that they played a part in the downfall of those legendary names. After making a brief stop in London to catch up with my family I was only too delighted to be able to switch my ticket to British Airways for the remainder of the journey.

After my year in Canada in the 50s I had been so impressed with the country that I had every intention of returning as an emigrant to seek a job with Trans Canada Airlines. Britons were welcome then and indeed it was the very flood of

G-OOOD still in Air 2000 guise but registered as C-FXOD
on the inaugural flight to Grenada and St Lucia.

those abandoning the UK that cooled my own enthusiasm for the idea. Toronto had since become one of the most multicultural cities in the world so it was a bit of a shock to find that the Brits were now apparently amongst the least welcome in Canada.

In immigration we were grilled about why we were coming to Canada to work. Pete was asked,

'Why isn't a Canadian doing this training?'

'Because there isn't a Canadian qualified to train on the B757.'

This being incontrovertible, we were allowed in after the modest outlay of $50 Canadian for a work permit. We settled into the Airport Hilton to find Angus Kinnear in residence as the new managing director.

We also found that our troubles were only just beginning. Charter airlines in Canada in the late 80s were very much the poor relations of the scheduled carriers. They tended to operate Douglas DC8s so clapped out that they were nicknamed 'Diesel 8s'. According to some of our new colleagues who had flown them, service, equipment and maintenance were at basic levels. So perhaps it was not surprising that there was apparently great political opposition to the idea of a British airline daring to break into the Canadian market and threatening existing companies by using shiny new aircraft, giving promises of a much superior product. The opposition to British participation from the National Transport Agency was particularly ironic given that one of the UK's biggest charter airlines, Britannia, was part of the Canadian Thomson Organisation.

Air 2000 was denied a licence to operate so, while we cooled our heels in the hotel, behind the scenes great machinations went on to change the official mindset. John Lecky, the new president of the airline, even took the aeroplane up to Ottawa on a combined publicity stunt and lobbying exercise. We filled the time with a bit of exploration and social meetings with the pilots we hoped to train. Pete and I hired a car to visit Niagara Falls and Centralia where I had trained on Harvards. It was rather sad to see the reduced status of the tarmac which had once boasted those serried ranks of bright yellow trainers.

The new airline's pilots included some interesting characters. Ted Ryczko had a sideline as firearms consultant to the Ontario Police. When we were invited to dinner at his house he showed us an arsenal which included every gun we had ever seen in the movies. Canada may not have the addiction to guns which so dominates USA politics but hunting is still a national sport. He gave us the opportunity to play with all of them, from the Colt .45 revolver and Winchester 73 rifle to repeater shotguns which fired those massive rounds often seen wreaking havoc in modern movies. It was impossible to imagine having such an experience back home.

Another group invited Pete and me to lunch at the innocuously but aptly named 'Airstrip'. We discovered we had been set up. Pete later congratulated me on managing to maintain an air of relatively cool academic interest while an extremely attractive but completely unclothed young lady performed a very athletic dance for my personal entertainment.

At last, after two weeks of uncertainty, a deal was struck in Ottawa – but it involved the relinquishing of any British control. So it was on 1 December 1988 that the first flight eventually departed. Canadian duty hour limitations were a lot less restrictive than those operating under British Civil Aviation rules. This first commercial flight was a round trip to Grenada and St Lucia which involved a duty day of nearly 16 hours.

It was a pleasure to be the supervising pilot with Dusty Thompson and Peter de Tracy but the first snag was encountered at security. The jobsworth in charge was dissatisfied with my Air 2000 UK ID badge which had been accepted at many other international airports. He insisted I should have ID specific for Lester Pearson Airport. However, after I pointed out that it took about three months to get the necessary security clearance for one of those precious documents and that the flight could not proceed without my supervision, the rest of the crew were able to persuade him that I was not a security threat.

It was interesting to arrive at Grenada shortly after it had been hit by Hurricane Gilbert. It might have been a mere Category 3 but the light aircraft area was still a scene of devastation.

The new airline's planned route structure provided an enjoyable opportunity to sample other parts of the aviation world and add to my collection of interesting destinations. These were the usual favourite choices of the Canadian winter tourist in Florida, Mexico and the Caribbean. We were the first airline to operate a B757 into St Kitts -- although the thrust required to negotiate the sloping tarmac posed something of a threat to the parked private aircraft!

On the whole, the start up period went very smoothly with only the occasional hiccup. One such occurred on a round trip via the Mexican island of Cozumel to nearby Cancun on the Yucatan peninsula. The passenger numbers out of Cozumel were a lot fewer than we expected but that was explained after we landed at Cancun. A somewhat embarrassed message from Cozumel explained that the missing numbers had now turned up. Fortunately the two airports are close enough for us to be able to return and rescue them without exceeding the generous Canadian duty time regulations.

Thus began a period of rapid expansion for the airline. Although it had to be renamed as Canada 3000 to emphasise the break from British influence, the new

The tarmac scene at Grenada in December 1988 after Hurricane Gilbert .

Captain Dusty Thompson (first left) with some of his Canada 3000 cabin crew. Training Captain Steve James of Air 2000 on the right.

service model proved extremely successful. Within ten years it was carrying two and a half million passengers on a fleet of over fifty aeroplanes to twenty-two different countries. By 10 September 2001, there were a record number of bookings for the looming holiday season. The very next day has gone down in the annals of infamy simply as 9/11. The destruction of the Twin Towers saw airline bookings collapse around the world but for the staff and passengers of Canada 3000 the timing just before the peak winter season was disastrous. The airline's rapid expansion had left it $260 million in debt and all rescue measures were too little, too late. The company filed for bankruptcy on 8 November 2001 leaving its crews and 50,000 passengers stranded at airports around the network.

But all seemed set fair on 20 December 1988 as Pete and I boarded the BA Toronto–London B747 to be home for Christmas. Thanks to a jet stream of nearly 200 knots the flying time was a remarkably short 5.45 hours. The full significance of that did not strike until the next day. On Wednesday, 21 December 1988 the world reacted with horror to the news that a Pan Am Flight 103 had been brought down by a bomb over the little Scottish town of Lockerbie and 270 innocent people had died. But for the fact that the flight had been delayed, the site of the accident might well have been over the sea, which was presumably the intention. An important factor in reducing the distance covered before the explosion was that the jet stream was still strong and the headwind component would have had a considerable negative effect on the flight's speed over the ground.

More significantly for Lockerbie, it was these strong westerlies that brought major portions of the wreckage far enough east to fall on the town. Otherwise they would have fallen on relatively uninhabited terrain.

Air 2000

In his 1988 budget, Nigel Lawson caused outrage on the Labour front bench by slashing taxes. Alex Salmond of the Scottish National Party was ejected from the chamber for declaring this to be 'an obscenity'. On the contrary, the chancellor's bold move was to prove a fine demonstration of the effects of the Laffer curve which suggests that lower taxes can actually produce higher revenue through

G-OOOG making a stop at Prestwick in July 1989 so that the flight to Bangor could start from Scotland's only 'trans-Atlantic' airport of the time!

encouraging enterprise and productivity. In particular the marginal rate of income tax was cut from 60% to 40%, less than half of what it had been under the previous Labour government.

Neil Burrows got in touch to suggest that it might now be worthwhile for Pete and me to work full time for Air 2000. I was particularly attracted by the fact that the airline had a base in Glasgow where my commercial aviation career had begun thirty years before.

So we both agreed to become employees again – so long as we were not required to be training pilots. Summer is the busy time for European charter airline pilots so most of the training and checking is done in the quieter winter months. We did not mind the expected heavy summer programme but drew the line at following it with an intensive winter training agenda. Neil accepted that while knowing that we could still have some educational input as line pilots.

For our official training swansong, we returned to the luxury of Singapore in the spring of 1989 to do a few conversion courses for new recruits to the airline. After completing the obligatory three landings to refresh our own recency licence requirements, the next step for me was reporting to Glasgow at the beginning of May as the Scottish holiday season got into summer swing. I had bought myself a little modern flat in Langside in the south of Glasgow. This was in recognition of the fact that night flying was a major part of the charter pilot's life. With a flat to myself I could arrange my sleeping patterns accordingly without disrupting the family routine at home.

After the impersonality of Heathrow and Gatwick it was a pleasure to be working within a relatively small base where most people were soon on first name terms. My arrival caused a little frisson of alarm among the senior captains, suspecting (erroneously) that I had perhaps been parachuted in to be put in charge. It was soon made clear that I had no power ambitions at all and was happy to enjoy life as a line pilot. In particular it was a joy to fly with the Glasgow cabin crew who worked hard but partied just as hard. It confirmed my view that esprit de corps on board was greatly improved when pilots and flight attendants operated as one team over each duty period.

The work pattern was the standard holiday charter mix of Mediterranean and Canary Islands flights. Re-visiting old haunts in the Med brought home how much aerial pollution had worsened since the early 60s. The joys of airborne sightseeing had been greatly reduced, particularly when looking up-sun. On terra firma pollution is most obvious when ostensibly clear skies turn grey rather than azure blue. Sometimes, sun-seekers complain that it takes much longer than expected to achieve the hoped-for depth of tan.

Apart from the large proportion of night flights and the fact that Glasgow was a bit further from the hotspots, in some ways the workload was easier than it had been in BA short haul. Charter pilots believed that they worked much harder than the pampered prima donnas of BA but the usual day's work was just two sectors, whether it be a short return flight to Minorca or a long outing to Cyprus or Tenerife. In BA short-haul, the normal day had been three or four sectors with night stops often involving either a very late arrival or a very early start at outstations. While a four sector day did not always involve a night stop, four experiences of the hassle of Heathrow made for a tiring duty.

However, dramatic changes were afoot as Air 2000 took full advantage of the long haul potential of the 757 to embark on trans-Atlantic flights to Florida and the Caribbean. Trans-oceanic flying had previously been considered to be the province of three- or four-engined aircraft, especially the latter in the piston engine era. The requirement of the time that twin-engined aircraft had to be within an hour's flying time of an alternate in the event of engine failure severely restricted routing choice. But new big fanjets like the Rolls Royce RB211s had proved so reliable that the regulatory authorities were considering relaxing the restriction.

Failures had been more common on piston engines and having four of them had not necessarily solved the problems. Pushing the power up on the remaining three put additional strain on those huge power plants with their pistons vibrating back and forth. There was a strong possibility that this could lead to further failure. The modern fanjets spun smoothly on their axes and did not seem unduly stressed if power had to be increased after a failure.

For Glasgow, however, there was a further complication. The slower Stratocruisers, Constellations and DC7s of old had found it something of a challenge to cross the Atlantic westwards against the prevailing winds. It had been standard practice to call at Prestwick to fill up before embarking on a crossing. In fact there was apparently a notice in the BOAC office at Prestwick in the 40s which stated that aircraft on the North Atlantic should be filled to full tanks 'unless the captain requests extra fuel!'

This was not as daft as it sounds. If the aircraft was allowed to stand for an hour or so with full tanks, the settling effect in the wings might allow for perhaps another hundred gallons to be added. That might make all the difference as far as completing the crossing was concerned. On the other side, stops at Gander, Goosebay or Halifax were also often required before continuing to Boston and New York. Although the need for them gradually reduced with the advent of the big jets, in 1978 the Labour

Government's Air Traffic Distribution Rules had led to Prestwick being designated as the only trans-Atlantic airport for Scotland

But the B757 was in a different league to the three and four engined aircraft that had traditionally plied the Atlantic. Its sparkling take-off performance meant it did not need Prestwick's long runway. Its range with a full load of 228 was not normally sufficient to make Orlando, Florida westbound against the prevailing winds so the standard plan was to refuel at the relatively quiet Bangor, Maine. Eastbound it was usually possible to fly Orlando–Glasgow without a stop.

But when Air 2000 applied for a trans-Atlantic licence out of Glasgow it encountered stern opposition from the Secretary of State for Defence in the Conservative government, George Younger, who just happened to be the MP for Ayr. It was ruled that aircraft would first have to land at Prestwick before proceeding. During the period when this masterpiece of bureaucratic thinking was being applied, pilots had a bit of fun seeing how quickly they could fly from Glasgow Abbotsinch to Glasgow Prestwick. My own figure was nine minutes but there were unconfirmed reports of the record being seven.

However, it was a very expensive farce. In 1989, Air 2000 resorted twice to the courts for permission to operate direct from Glasgow. By 1990 George Younger had left the cabinet and the new Secretary of State for Transport, Cecil Parkinson, declared an 'open skies' policy which ended Prestwick's 43-year-old monopoly. Airlines were given permission to operate trans-Atlantic from any Scottish airport they chose.

It does not require a close study of politics to understand why this victory for common sense was not greeted with unalloyed joy by some of the politicians concerned. Ayrshire Labour MP George Ffoulkes claimed the decision 'defied logic' and would pose an environmental threat to Scottish cities with increased danger to their inhabitants. Dark reference was made to Lockerbie.

Unsurprisingly, George Younger remained defiant claiming that,

> 'No convincing financial arguments have been produced by the business lobby in Glasgow in support of their case and no operational arguments have been produced favouring Glasgow over Prestwick.' [1]

John Swinney, transport spokesman for the Scottish National Party at the time, conformed to his party's Pavlovian reaction to any ruling from Westminster by branding the decision 'short-sighted, destructive and anti-Scottish!' Fortunately that was not the view of the Scottish business community, nor of the nine other airlines

1 *Glasgow Herald,* 7 March 1990.

which promptly applied for permission to operate out of Abbotsinch. Nearly thirty years later it is impossible to quantify the subsequent boost to the Scottish economy.

Trans-Atlantic passengers are sometimes mystified as to why they find themselves as far north as Greenland when they are heading for places like Florida. Mercator flat maps in particular give a misleading impression. To understand why Great Circle routes are the shortest it is only necessary to stretch a piece of string between two points on a globe of the world. It immediately becomes obvious that Florida and the Caribbean are closer to Glasgow than London. In the days of the sailing ships, that had given Glasgow an important advantage in the import of sugar and tobacco.

Bangor International Airport, located close to the northern boundary of Maine, was the first American airport on the Great Circle routing from Europe to the Eastern seaboard of the States and the Caribbean.

Equipped with a massive runway capable of handling the largest aircraft, it had been a USAF military airfield and was still home to National Guard and refuelling aircraft. Thanks to the B757, the little town was to enjoy a heyday of commercial activity in the 80s and 90s as restrictions were eased on twin-engine aircraft operations across the Atlantic. The previous requirement for twin-engine aircraft to have suitable alternates within an hour's flying time meant that their Atlantic crossings had to route close to Iceland, Greenland and the traditional boltholes of Goosebay and Gander in Canada. In view of the demonstrated reliability of the new big fanjet engines, that restriction was eased to two and eventually three hours. To British charter airlines equipping with brand new B757s this was a gift from the

Air 2000 B757 G-OOOI at Bangor, Maine in 1991.

gods. They had an aeroplane that could carry two thirds of the passenger load of a four-engined B747 but burn half the fuel. Sun-hungry but cost-conscious Brits could now be offered access to Florida and the Caribbean at reasonable prices.

Under the new relaxed rules, Monarch had the honour of operating the first trans-Atlantic 757 charter flight on 1 May 1988. But Air Europe and Air 2000 were hot on their heels. Although Glasgow flights could usually operate direct from Orlando that was not always the case for Gatwick and Manchester and was never scheduled from Montego Bay in Jamaica. Soon Bangor airport hotels had a steady clientele of airline slip crews as routes branched out to the sunspots. The airline also had the flexibility of using whichever crew was best available for the return flight.

Thus Bangor became the favoured place to catch up with colleagues from the other Air 2000 bases which were operating similar patterns to our own. The town also became the scene of some determined bargain hunting as cabin crew discovered the joys of American mall prices. Their joy was unconfined when night stops in Orlando further widened the choice available. Not that the pilots were immune from shopping fever. In the 80s sports such as golf and tennis were regarded as pursuits of the rich in the UK. Prices in America could be a third or a half of those back home. There was a steady trade in barbeques being loaded as crew baggage on return flights although, strangely, more often to Gatwick or Manchester than Glasgow.

Some were even more adventurous. My old Tiger Club colleague Pete Jarvis was flying for our rivals Air Europe. He managed to import a beautiful classic Chevrolet Corvette which was to win him more than one Concours d' Elegance. While that could not be squeezed into a B757 hold, he did have more success with a classic Triumph motor bike!

For those of us not completely devoted to shopping, there were other opportunities. Light aviation is considered to be an activity of the idle rich in the UK with the corresponding burden of pricing, regulation and bureaucracy. In North America it was just a part of ordinary life. The difference had been clearly brought home to me on a previous holiday in New England. My wife and I had been relaxing by Lake Winnipesaukee in New Hampshire when a couple of floatplanes landed, taxied to the shore and moored by the banks. The occupants disembarked and, to my great amusement, casually started fishing. It was difficult to imagine that happening back home without generating complaint or legal sanction.

This experience triggered an idea in the back of my mind. Lake Pushaw, only a few miles from Bangor, was home to a small float plane company where the rate for lessons was an absolute bargain compared to the UK equivalent. For pilots keen to

Learning to land on water at Lake Pushaw, Maine 1990.

explore another aspect of the wonderful world of aviation it proved the ideal way to pass the odd standover day. My co-pilot was usually just as keen to join in.

Most of our training was on Lake Pushaw, which had a generous length more than adequate for water take-offs (which in some water conditions can be protracted). On one occasion, however, our instructor decided to allow a landing on a smaller adjacent lake. Not only smaller but surrounded by quite high trees. For take-off he re-assessed the situation and decided he had better do it. As we roared across the lake the occasional problems of un-sticking from the water surface became ominously obvious. As the trees loomed closer and closer I remember thinking that if we did come to grief, at least it would not be my duty to explain to Neil Burrows what had happened to one of his cockpit crews!

The old cliché is that travel broadens the mind and most of our passengers crossing the pond for the first time were deeply appreciative of the opportunities they now had. Occasionally we were shocked that a minority grasped so little of the scale and geography of their journey. Halfway across to Bangor one day a passenger asked about our position.

'Halfway across the ocean,' was my statement of the blindingly obvious.

But the next question was a sorry comment on the decline of the once legendary Scottish educational system.

'Which ocean?'

But that paled into insignificance compared to a Manchester passenger on a sub-charter we were doing for Airtours – a company at the value end of the market (not to be confused with British Airtours). Their passengers had been asked to complete questionnaires on their holidays and naturally our cabin crew could not resist the opportunity to take a peek. They brought one up for our edification which read: 'I thought £150 was too much for a fortnight in Jamaica!'

That price could only have been part of a last-minute fire sale. Leaving aside the 20 hours flying time, could the dissatisfied customer have had a fortnight in Blackpool for a similar amount? It tended to confirm a possibly apocryphal story from the travel trade that some UK holiday makers in the Caribbean had complained at the unfairness of American passengers being able to get home in three hours while it took them ten.

For all the benefits the aeroplane has brought travelling millions around the world, it has also permitted a minority to do untold damage to other cultures. Even in the expensive jet-setting days of the sixties there were those who thought that seeing the world consisted of a circumnavigation via American luxury hotel chains. The advent of cheap mass travel allowed those interested only in sun, sea, sex and booze to demand that the world change to suit them. Thus countries with strong religious customs such as Spain and Cyprus had to abandon their conservative traditions in pursuit of tourist wealth. Their initial resistance to beach bikinis – never mind beach nudity – is now largely forgotten. Beach hotels proliferate and native cuisine gives way to fish and chips, pizza and foreign beers.

That was brought home to me on one night flight into Corfu for Club 18-30 – a club seemingly dedicated to cramming as much alcohol and sex as possible into a week or two. Bear in mind that Byron was a hero to Greece and inspired wide respect for Britain. That was particularly true of Corfu where there is even a tradition of playing cricket. When our local agent entered the flight deck he greeted us with a question:

'Why do you bring these people to my island?'

It was difficult to disagree with him. A loutish minority had not only ruined a corner of Corfu but also destroyed Britain›s image in many other international tourist hotspots. The insistence in some American states on providing ID proof of being over twenty-one did something to curb Britain's easy approach to teenage drinking.

By and large, westbound trans-Atlantic flights operate in daylight. Clocks on the East coast are five hours behind those in the UK and flight times are usually less than seven hours. Passengers therefore arrive only two hours local time after departure with useful daylight still available. The downside for crews is that return flights are usually overnight. However much they attempt to adjust to local time by delaying going to bed after arrival, their body clocks usually find them wide awake by four in the morning. It can be difficult to get sufficient rest to prepare for the night ahead -- particularly for the young and active. As I approached sixty that was less of a problem for me provided I could have a couple of hours in the afternoon before pick-up.

Night flying has its own magical moments of compensation. Great cities such as New York and London are magnificent spectacles at night. Seven miles up, the darkened cockpit provides grandstand views of the night sky which are denied to city dwellers below. The planets and myriads of stars stand out clearly and it is much easier to pick up the moving light of a satellite or space station. Over Canada, the Northern Lights can be spectacularly true to their Scottish nickname 'the Merry Dancers'.

The downside is that flying East at altitude means encountering the dawn a couple of hours before those earthbound at destination. The first warning is usually given by Sirius, the Dog Star. Sirius is the brightest star in the heavens and as it rises often seems to change colour as seen through the earth›s atmosphere. So much so that its flicker has been confused with aircraft navigation lights – or even reported as a UFO.

The sun itself appears just as pilots' eyes are at their grittiest and provides a stern head-on test of the effectiveness of sunglasses until descent can be commenced into cloud cover. Some of our flights into Glasgow from Orlando spared us that problem by arriving in the middle of the night. For one who had known the era of candles and oil lamps, it was a revelation to fly over the Hebrides at three in the morning and see how many street lamps the islands boasted.

The Mustang

Standover days in Orlando provided further evidence of different attitudes to flying between our two countries. Readers who recall the beginning of this book will re-member that it was the sight of a Spitfire that fired the seven-year-old me with the im-probable ambition of becoming a pilot. Ever since, I had dreamed that one day I might get to fly one myself. There were twin seat Spits available in England which seemed to offer the most likely chance of achieving the dream. When I rang up for details I was told that the cost was £2,000 for twenty minutes. While that seemed excessive in the early 1990s, it was not the real deal-breaker. No, that came when the pilot said,

'I do the take-off and the landing and, if you want to see some aerobatics, I can show you that too.'

Crazy Horse: *Lee Lauderbeck in the front cockpit with
the author in the rear. Kissimmee, December 1991.*

My interest cooled rapidly.

'Just a minute. You want me to pay £2,000 to watch you fly a Spitfire?'

The contrast with the American attitude could not have been more marked. Glasgow co-pilot, Derek Macphail, was actually involved in the re-build of a North American P51 Mustang. The Mustang was arguably even more important than the Spitfire to the success of the allies in WWII. Its extra range compared to its predecessor made it possible to provide cover for raids in Germany and thereby considerably reduce the dreadful losses among the bomber crews.

It was Derek who pointed out that Mustang training was available at Kissimmee airport near Orlando. On a Florida trip we did together in December 1991 he kindly introduced me to Lee Lauderbeck of the company Stallion 51 which actually runs Mustang training courses. The difference in pricing structure was incredible. For $750 (about £500 at the time) I could have a comprehensive pre-flight briefing, thirty minutes flying and a video of the flight at the end of it. But it was the American can-do attitude which was really remarkable. Lee made clear he expected me to do most of the flying and opened his very detailed briefing with:

'Bill, I want you to fly this aeroplane as aggressively as you know how!'

The first sight of the aeroplane itself would have gladdened the heart of any pilot. *Crazy Horse* was so immaculately prepared that even the inside of the undercarriage doors had been polished to a mirror-like sheen. My time in Canada 35 years earlier bore fruit as the cockpit was reasonably similar to that of the Harvard. Hardly surprising really as both iconic aircraft were among famous products of the old North American Aviation company. Little wonder that the Harvard had served as introduction to so many American military planes.

I was allowed to do the take-off and explore the delightful handling. Lee did a couple of aeros and then I had a go. Twenty plus years absence from sporting flying in propeller driven aircraft took its inevitable toll on the accuracy of my attempts (jet pilots tend to forget the importance of rudder in aerobatics). My stomach had also lost its previous imperviousness to changing aerobatic forces – although, fortunately for me, not to the point of embarrassment! Lee demonstrated how the P51 had also been used in ground attack roles before we returned to Kissimmee so I could shoot a couple of landings.

We had so much fun that the thirty minutes had mysteriously extended to fifty but, incredibly, there was no mention of an increased fee. The contrast with the potential Spitfire venture could not have been starker. An unforgettable experience.

In the spring of 1992 there was dramatic change to my family life when my wife was diagnosed with a serious cancer. Neil Burrows overrode the station

Montego Bay, June 1992. Airport security, Jamaica style pre 9/11.

crewing plan to transfer me down to Gatwick to be closer to my Surrey home. Barring blockages on the M25, the commuting time from Molesey to Gatwick was almost exactly the same as it had been to the much closer Heathrow in my BA incarnation.

Gatwick was a much larger base but the Air 2000 team spirit still prevailed. The route mix now had some longer flights which would not have been possible from Glasgow. These included return trips to Luxor in Egypt and Banjul in the Gambia. The latter, being close to a fourteen hour duty day with twelve hours airborne, was particularly sensitive to any delays. More civilised was a trip to the Maldives which involved the crew in a night-stop in Bahrain in order to operate Bahrain-Malé-Bahrain the next day. Descending over the coral atolls of the Indian Ocean on the way into Malé made a very pleasant change from our regular Mediterranean haunts. At only two metres above sea level the airport itself is one of the lowest in the world.

The real plum trip though was a tour to Mombasa in Kenya via Athens. As it operated only once a week, the crew had little option but to night-stop for six days between services. Mombasa at the time was a very pleasant city with fine hotels, restaurants and beaches. Crews had no difficulty in bearing this unusual departure from the normal hectic work schedule with remarkable fortitude. The increasing frequency of airline schedules render such bonuses much less likely today.

Some passengers, however, had a rather different understanding of duty time limitations. The flight left Gatwick about 7 p.m. of a winter's evening, stopped at Athens to re-fuel about 11 p.m. and then flew on through the African night to arrive in the heat and humidity of a Kenyan morning about 9 a.m. In those days there was no real air traffic control or radar coverage between Egypt and Kenya so pilots transmitted their height and position blind and kept sharp ears on international frequencies for other traffic. After this twelve-hour-duty night, we trailed into the steaming heat of immigration and customs after the passengers, thinking wistfully of showers and bed.

A passenger kindly inquired whether we were going straight back!

All too soon, in 1993 my 60th birthday loomed. In the 1990s that was the compulsory retirement date for airline pilots in most countries. In the States, co-pilots over 60 were permitted but not captains. As pilots of that age still have to pass medicals and competency checks every six months there was no real logic to this ruling other than to offer co-pilots a better chance of command. Nowadays, all pilots can fly to 65 so long as they can pass the relevant six-monthly checks. For my last long-haul tour I requested and was given a four-day trip to Bangor and Florida

At Tenerife on the author's last trip in command for Air 2000 on 17 September 1993.

out of Glasgow. In gratitude for my Mustang experience, I particularly asked that Derek Macphail be the co-pilot.

At Bangor there was the usual mix of crew from the other bases and, thanks to Richard Hatswell from Gatwick, there was a surprise farewell party. A couple of nights later we were able to operate direct from Orlando to arrive in Glasgow at 6.05 a.m. after seven hours and twenty minutes.

Thanks to daylight and fine weather, my actual last trip for Air 2000 on 17 September 1993 was a not-too-taxing Gatwick–Tenerife–Gatwick . After a small farewell party a couple of weeks later, I retired for the third and presumably last time.

Alitalia

The apparent end of my airline career allowed plenty of time for other things. With Linda's illness in remission we enjoyed the longest holiday of our married life, a five-week tour of Australia and New Zealand. There was more time for Gaelic media activities and I started a project of translating the work of one of South Uist's outstanding poets, Donald John MacDonald.

Boeing 767 300ER at Rome Fiumicino.

Towards the end of 1994 we attended an Air 2000 get-together near Gatwick. Despite the unforced jollity, we heard that recent results had suffered since the Gulf War of 1992. There were also rumours that Neil Burrows might be leaving. The accuracy of the rumours was confirmed when Pete rang me a couple of months later. The Australian company Nordstress (part of Ansett Worldwide Leasing) was setting up a contract with Alitalia to operate some of their American and African services with a pair of long range Boeing 767-300ERs. Neil was to be the flight operations director. To comply with EU regulations the pilots had to hold European licences. Would we be interested in doing the training?

As the wide-bodied B767 has a cockpit almost identical to that of the narrow-bodied B757 this was a most attractive idea. The two aircraft had been designed from the outset to be operated in common. Thanks to the aforementioned USA ban on captains over 60, we would not be able to operate the commercial services in command but that was not a problem for the preliminary training.

However, we had reckoned without the bureaucracy of the Civil Aviation Agency in London. They pointed out it was more than five years since we had last carried out licence simulator checks on other pilots and our authority had lapsed. For it to be renewed we would have to repeat the Instrument Examiner's course. This could be arranged for the modest sum of £35,000.

The absurdity of it was breathtaking. We had both been practising authorised examiners for twenty years. In my case, I had been one of only two BA pilots who had actually conducted in-house training courses for our own examiners. As mentioned earlier, new examiners tend to focus on nit-picking detail whereas the more experienced favour the broad brush of 'would I allow my family to fly with this pilot?'. The CAA expected us to spend a fortnight at vast expense being re-trained in the nit-picking detail by someone with possibly only a fraction of our airline experience.

There was no question of the new project paying such sums. Neil would still like to have us but on the understanding that we could only operate as co-pilots. Attractive though the thought of working in Rome was, my experience of ex-captains acting as co-pilots had not been a positive one. With some regret, I turned the proposition down. We did not need the money and I was busy with lots of non-aviation stuff. My captain's four bars had been hard won and I was reluctant to lose one.

However, Neil could be very persuasive. He knew that some of his co-pilots would have minimum qualifications and that some of his captains were an unknown quantity. A bit of experience in the right-hand seat would be a very good thing for the contract. It may sound childish but his clinching offer was that we could still wear captain's uniform. On previous visits to Italian friends I had already noticed their love and respect for titles such as *Dottore* or *Signor Enginiere*. It had to be admitted that *Commandante* had a certain ring to it! More practically, it would carry more weight with Alitalia staff travel when it came to commuting home for days off.

Thus a varied band of pilots found ourselves in April 1995 settling into the *Residenza Aurelia Antica* in the outskirts of Rome. The accommodation of self-catering apartments was well suited to the inconvenient working hours of commercial aviation. Much as we keenly appreciated the opportunity of living in one of Europe's most famous cities, we had forgotten that Rome weather at Easter is not much better than that of the UK. The Residence had a swimming pool but it was not even due to be filled till July. We gathered that July was also the month when Roman matrons would feel it safe to shed their fur coats. We were a mixture of ex-BA and ex-charter pilots with occasional temporary reinforcement from current Air 2000 crews. The full-time management team supporting Neil already included Alan Blake and Keith Castle, with whom I had operated the first Air 2000 commercial flight. The cabin attendants were a varied and interesting bunch drawn from the Italian speaking communities of Australia and New Zealand.

In the 1970s we had had a family holiday visiting friends in Umbria. Thanks to them we had been introduced to some members of the Italian professional middle class. In Britain at the time their equivalents were under the cosh of the punitive tax rates mentioned in a previous chapter. Holiday hotspots were the playgrounds of those beneficiaries of Britain's thriving black economy: bricklayers, plumbers, electricians etc. who could demand payment in cash. Back then BEA captains such as myself had salaries of around £7,000 per annum, which was very respectable for the time. However, some married to cabin crew found their other halves had an equivalent take-home pay simply because more of their remuneration was in tax-free allowances.

The contrast in Italy was stark. It became clear that paying tax was regarded at the time as more of a voluntary activity. We were entertained by a dentist whose luxury flat was furnished with expensive antiques set off by genuine old masters on the walls. The highlight was an invitation to dinner at the home of a doctor. His villa sat in its own vineyards, the delicious product of which was much enjoyed when twenty of us sat down to an excellent meal. Afterwards his cook took a well-deserved round of applause.

There was a downside of course. Kidnapping for ransom was an ever-present threat in Italy. *Dottore's* vineyard was surrounded by an electric fence and two Alsatians roamed the grounds.

These middle class expectations still affected Alitalia in the 90s. As the national airline of Italy, it had struggled to adapt to the changing economics of the industry. Continuing losses had required frequent government support even though that was supposedly not permitted by EU legislation. The permanent staff still enjoyed salaries and pensions on early retirement more appropriate to the golden days of the past.

In the circumstances, we expected to be deeply resented as a threat to that comfortable lifestyle. It has to be said that, but for an initial token protest, we were treated with civility and good manners. True, it had been agreed that our contract was a temporary fix until the airline could mount the necessary training and staff to take over the crewing of our two Boeing 767-300s. These were long range aircraft so the bulk of the work would be trans-Atlantic to New York, Boston and Chicago. All of these schedules were approximately two hours longer than they would be out of London. On the other hand, Rome was closer to Africa, so destinations such as Nairobi, Lagos, Accra and Dakar together with Dubai and Jeddah in the Middle East were more accessible. The wide body B767s were considerably larger than their single aisle B757 sister ships so our 180-seat, mixed-class configuration offered passengers spacious luxury compared to the 233 seats by then common on charter B757s. British holiday B767s carried nearly 300.

After jumping through all the usual hoops with regard to medical and licensing requirements, my first flight was to Nairobi via Jeddah in Saudi Arabia. At the latter the cabin crew had to go through the usual farce of concealing any evidence of alcohol consumption on board prior to inspection by the religious police. When one triumphantly discovered an empty miniature bottle, I was sent to make the usual apology with insincere promises of ensuring it would not happen again.

At Nairobi we were the first Alitalia B767 arrival so found, much to our surprise, that we were expected at a press conference. Such are not popular with pilots but, in view of my media experience, my captain informed me I had drawn the short straw. At least my flash new uniform came into its own.

As the service was twice weekly we had a couple of pleasant days at the Windsor Golf Club Hotel before the 10.45 p.m. pick-up for the return flight. Jeddah's huge airport was still busy in the middle of the night but the transit sticks in mind for one telling incident. Just before we were due to close the doors, a large Mercedes drew up by the steps and disgorged several female first-class passengers clad head to foot in impenetrable black burqas. After take-off the cabin crew reported that as soon as the seat belts sign was switched off they all vanished into the loos – only to re-emerge in the jeans and T-shirts appropriate for their shopping trip to Rome.

As the service settled in we found we had been moved to another splendid hotel: the Safari Park outside Nairobi. As the name suggests, the accommodation was arranged in separate African-themed buildings and the hotel boasted of more than half a dozen restaurants of various international cuisines. It happened that I was on the first Alitalia crew to stay there and found we had an official reception to meet the senior management. The Dutch head chef told us he needed 200 staff to run the varied catering on offer. When it was suggested that must be a challenging number to supervise, he merely pointed out his previous appointment in Shanghai had required over 400. More illuminating was a discussion with another Kenyan senior manager, forthright in dissatisfaction with the country's politicians. Corruption was endemic while not enough was being done for the tourist trade - such a vital a part of the Kenyan economy

They were happy to tell us that the Italian restaurant had been warned to expect our arrival. Now Rome is an enchanting city but in the 1990s there was very little penetration by the international ethnic cuisines which are so popular with Brits. Yes, we all loved Italian food but we could not pass up the chance to sample the delights of the hotel's Chinese, Japanese, Indian and African restaurants.

Our other African flight was to Accra in Ghana via Lagos in Nigeria. The two airports are separated by a short flight over Togo and Benin but the contrast between them was stark. By comparison with Lagos, Accra airport was a model of efficiency. True there was still much evidence of poverty in the city but a Canadian businessman in the comfortable hotel expressed the view that Ghana was the best country for business in Africa.

Boston and New York were also regular destinations. For noise abatement reasons, the south easterly runway 13 Left at the latter's John F. Kennedy airport is notorious for requiring a turn very close to the airport to stabilise much lower than normal at about three hundred feet. It was a great pleasure to tick that off my bucket list.

Our longest flights were to Santo Domingo in the Caribbean and Chicago in the USA. Both involved between ten and eleven hours flying west-bound but usually less than ten on the return. Approaching old age had mellowed my youthful impatient metabolism to the point where I could enjoy the more leisurely tempo of long-haul flying. It is true that modern navigation equipment and much improved weather forecasting had considerably reduced the challenges of old. Our navigation computers were so accurate that aircraft on the same trans-Atlantic route at different levels would pass directly one over the other. So much so that it was often deemed safer to off-set a track by half a mile or so to reduce chance of mishap in the event of any mistake in levels or emergency descent.

With old age also comes less need for sleep. Provided I could have a couple of hours before tackling a return night flight, I found it easier to stay awake than some of my younger colleagues. Once upon a time, pilots had coped on a steady stream of coffees. That can be counter-productive due to the diuretic effect which can lead to dehydration and caffeine over-stimulation. The cabin crew at least appreciated my solution, which was to rely on a two-litre bottle of water with just one mug of tea before commencing descent in the morning. It is a regime to be recommended for any long-haul passenger who wishes to arrive at destination feeling as well as can be expected. The effect of alcohol is greatly increased in the low humidity, low pressure atmosphere of an aircraft cabin. Sadly it is best avoided if you wish to function efficiently on arrival!

While pilots have to be strictly disciplined in avoidance of pre-flight drinking, our lifestyle off-duty in Rome was too close to the care-free bachelor days in the RAF mess of yore. It was fatally easy to go out as a bunch and enjoy too much of the local wines with our meals. The effect was aggravated if we fell for the easy charm of 'just a night-cap' before retiring to bed.

It was the six-monthly medical that saved me. The examiner flagged up a serious rise in blood pressure, of which I would otherwise have been unaware. It was undoubtedly exacerbated by the regular commuting back to London to check up on my sick wife and matters at home – and also by the undoubted stress of acting as a co-pilot after all those years in charge. Reluctantly, it was time to leave Rome. Neil was very understanding about the loss of a pilot. My last rostered flight was for a Chicago night-stop. On 1 July 1996 I commuted back from London and next morning checked in for the Chicago flight with Barry Wood as captain.

Now those of you who have followed the ups and downs of the career recorded in these pages will be aware of the several retirements under my belt. But when I picked up the flight plan that day I felt that a supreme power was trying to tell me something. Trans-Atlantic routes change daily to take advantage of the most favourable wind patterns. The usual route from Rome was diagonally across France and well south of Ireland. Barry had graciously offered me this first leg and the flight plan read like a summary of my career. Our route followed the familiar high points of the old BEA hunting ground: Turin–Geneva–Paris–London–Glasgow–Benbecula! Even more extraordinarily, on the other side of the pond we were to fly directly over Centralia in Ontario where I had diced with the Harvard in the Canadian Air Force forty years before. It seemed like a clear warning that enough was enough!

True to plan, we flew directly over Benbecula so it seemed only right to call up for a weather report with our Alitalia call-sign. I could visualise a large question mark forming in the sky as they pondered the chances of a B767 arrival but the not-so-unusual feature of their July weather was that the temperature was 12 degrees Celsius. For comparison, at our Greenland alternate that day the temperature was 17 degrees.

After ten and a half hours we arrived on Chicago O' Hare's 09 Right runway. The landing was not one of my best but that was nothing to the sickening sensation when I reached into my brief case for my passport. For the first time in my life I had flown without it and I realised it must still be in the pocket of the jacket I had worn on the previous night's passenger flight. American immigration officials are notorious for their unbending application of the rules and I faced the possibility of being denied entry to the States and an ignominious return as passenger on the aircraft I had just flown in. Worse from the airline's point of view, there would be no co-pilot available to crew the return flight the next day.

To my amazement, the fates relented. As luck would have it, the immigration officer was a grizzled veteran who took pity on my abject misery and allowed me entry without the passport. It is true that immigration must have had a record of my many visits to the States over forty years but a younger man might not have had the bottle to exercise discretion. The next night, Barry flew us back to Rome and my aviation career came to an end.

My logbook records over 17,000 hours, most acquired in flights of less than two hours in over forty types. To that must be added many hundreds of hours in simulators while training, checking and being checked. Flying as a passenger does not count!

Fear of Flying

*I*n the years since WWII, commercial air travel has evolved from being considered a rather risky and expensive form of travel for the privileged to an economic form of mass transport which has opened up the world to the ordinary citizen in the street. The continual drive for technical improvement and efficiency has seen passenger numbers worldwide explode to the degree that in 2017 more than ten million passengers were carried by commercial airlines *each day*.

Despite the consequent congestion on airways and at airports, the really remarkable statistic is that the accompanying improvement in safety has made the commercial aeroplane by far the safest form of transport. As today's ten million hurtle through space seven miles above the surface at over 500 miles per hour, they are arguably safer than if they had stayed at home. Think about it. Ten million is more than the population of London or countries such as Hungary or Bulgaria. In any grouping of that size, a substantial number will meet with disaster in their own environment through drowning in the bath, falling down the stairs, being stabbed by a jealous lover or crashing on the way to the supermarket. Worldwide, 1.25 million die on the roads every year – over 3,000 every day.

By contrast, in the first six months of 2017 there were no fatal accidents at all recorded by the world's major airlines. That's right – zero! Despite that, it is estimated that up to 20% (or 1 in 5) of airline passengers suffer from a fear of flying. That could be over 80 passengers on a full B747.

That these fears are irrational is of little comfort to the sufferers. These are generally believed to fall into two main groups. Claustrophobics constitute the smaller number and presumably their dislike of being confined in small spaces with no means of escape is not restricted to aircraft fuselages. For the rest, an important factor seems to be that passenger flying entails a loss of personal control over their own destiny. There is some correlation with back-seat-driver syndrome but that would be an over-simplistic diagnosis.

One of the problems is the low level of awareness in the general public of the high professional standards within the industry. Fear-of-flying courses which improve technical knowledge can do much to calm nameless fears triggered by occasional noises or disturbances due to turbulence. In the days before cockpit visits fell victim to security concerns, it was often comforting for nervous passengers to see that the crew at least were completely relaxed about the operation.

Mind you, calmness in the cockpit could generate its own misconceptions. Frequently, disappointment was expressed that the autopilot being engaged meant that no-one was wrestling with the controls in true Hollywood fashion. In fact it was a condition of most cockpit visits that the autopilot *should* be engaged.

Air turbulence is perhaps the most common source of unease. At the very least it can be irritating if movement around the cabin is prohibited and service is restricted. At its worst it can be a frightening experience for the nervous passenger. It may help the latter if we consider some of the causes. Water and air both obey the laws of fluids but one is visible and the other is not. On a ship it is perfectly obvious why the vessel is pitching and rolling but turbulence in an aircraft can come literally out of the blue. We may think of air as being insubstantial but if you are moving through it at high speed it increasingly takes on the qualities of water. If a wind of 100 mph can blow down large trees it becomes easier to understand how the 400 tonne weight of a jumbo jet can be supported by air moving around its wings at much higher speeds. At jet speeds of up to 600 mph any disturbance or current in the air mass can have just as powerful an effect as anything at sea.

Vertically developing clouds of the cumulus family do give a visual indication of air movements. The least level of disturbance is normally in the low level stratocumulus typical of a summer afternoon when warm air rising reaches the point where cooler temperature causes its moisture content to condense out as cloud. The typical cobblestone effect is short-term on initial climb-out or approach. More vigorous vertical currents can produce the towering effect of cumulus castellanus and have a marked effect on passenger comfort. Fortunately their water content makes them visible to weather radar and pilots make every effort to avoid them.

When air masses become unstable due to moist air passing over heated ground surface we get the seething columns known as cumulonimbus. Their mixture of up and down currents can retain moisture to the point where heavy rain or hail is produced and the cloud becomes charged enough to produce lightning. Any transit through rapidly changing air currents makes for severe turbulence so pilots will give thunderclouds a very wide berth indeed. Fortunately they also show up quite clearly on weather radar. Notice that aeroplanes are often struck by lightning but the effect usually dissipates round the outside of the fuselage and any damage is rarely more than superficial.

Once you accept that air at high speed has all the force of water, clear air turbulence becomes easier to understand. Generally speaking, wind speeds are much higher aloft with the strongest currents being the jet streams such as that which flows eastwards across the Atlantic marking the boundary between hot and cold air masses. Just as in a fast river, the centre flow can be quite smooth even at speeds near 200 mph. But as you cross the edges of the stream there can be turbulence in eddies like those at the edges of a river where the flow is slowed. As passengers embark on longer and longer flights they are ever more likely to experience clear air turbulence at some stage of their journey. It is always worth heeding the advice from the crew that seat belts should remain fastened while seated. Similar clear air effects can be experienced close to the ground as wind speed is slowed by ground friction. The ensuing turbulence can be aggravated in cross winds by large buildings close to runway thresholds such as at Heathrow and Gatwick.

What can the pilot do to comfort the nervous? I always thought it worth saying something along the lines of:

'Ladies and gentlemen, I'm sorry if this turbulence is making life uncomfortable for you. I would like to reassure you that the aeroplane is perfectly comfortable with it. Those of you sitting near windows may notice that the wings flex in turbulence; they are designed to do that!'

It is true that aircraft wings flex in flight; more than twenty feet at the tip in some cases. The most obvious current example might be the Boeing 787. Its wings, heavy with thousands of gallons of fuel, curve upwards as they develop lift.

The pursuit of the cheapest fares has inevitably downgraded the passenger experience. Cramped seats, the end of free meals and drinks on shorter sectors, tedious security procedures and locked flight decks have all reduced the excitement of flight. We take it all so much for granted that drunken passengers have even been known to assault pilots, apparently oblivious of the fact that they are in an aluminium tube, seven miles up in the air travelling at over 500 miles per hour. In wide-bodied aircraft only a fraction of the passengers have window seats so the quality of the in-flight videos becomes a more important issue than any scenery below.

For my part, I never tired of the enchantment of sitting in the sharp-end seats with the best view. It would be immensely gratifying if this little book re-awakened something of that sense of awe and magic in the reader.

It was my great good fortune to spend my working life being paid to do a job which was also my hobby, during a period which saw the most incredible expansion in the industry. In particular, personal thanks must be given to Rolls Royce for the wonderful engines which so reliably powered all of the commercial aircraft I flew except for the first and last.

However, it has also been a period where the status of the airline pilot has been in continuous decline. Sadly, pilots were often their own worst enemies when it came to educating the public as to the real nature of the job. In the interest of reassuring the nervous, self deprecation became part of the stereotype. Comments like:

'We just press the button and the autopilot takes us there'

or

'The computer tells me we will be arriving at xxxx hours'

do scant justice to the many hours of training, checking and experience that go into the make-up of the average airline pilot. In 2018 Britain, it cost over £100,000 to train for the lowest level of commercial licence. Throughout a career an airline pilot has to pass regular simulator competency checks, line checks and medicals which give him or her up to five opportunities a year to lose the essential licence. Even the most senior pilots are required to demonstrate twice a year in the simulator their command of operational skills and emergency procedures. Most of us would agree we were still learning until the day we retired.

You do not have to be an intellectual to be a good airline pilot but you do require an unusual combination of qualities. These include: good qualifications in maths and physics; sound long-term physical health; good coordination and reactions; communication skills; and an ability to think in three dimensions. (Note that nowadays some train drivers operating in one dimension earn more than pilots for some smaller airlines). Not least is that indefinable quality we call 'bottle' which enables cool and logical thought in the stress of an emergency situation.

In the days when cockpit visits were allowed, it was always disappointing when an ostensibly educated passenger would visit the cockpit to tell us that we must be bored out of our minds as we had nothing to do any more. Leaving aside the rudeness of expressing such sentiments on entering someone else's professional environment, it was sad commentary on the inadequacy of general technical knowledge even among the better informed. It does help to explain the poor quality of most media comment on aviation matters.

It is true that modern airliners are well equipped with computers. These computers permit two pilots to manage aeroplanes many times larger and faster than early transports such as the Hastings which had a cockpit crew of five. Specifically, navigators, wireless operators and flight engineers have been replaced by black boxes. However, these computers are moving through space at nearly 600 miles an hour and there is no 'pause' button. If pilots allow their thinking to lag behind them, all on board could be in serious trouble.

'Do your computers run your office?'

Of course, developments in automation are geared towards removing manual control from the equation. In some modern aircraft, disengaging the autopilot merely means that the pilot is directly controlling the autopilot rather than having a human connection to the control surfaces. While the sort of eccentric behaviour mentioned in the early chapters of this book would not be tolerated nowadays it is sad that bureaucracy mushrooms in an attempt to curb any individuality at all.

Concerns have arisen that many modern co-pilots have not had the breadth of raw experience enjoyed by their predecessors and will not have the same opportunity to hone their skills before reaching command. But however much autopilot designers attempt to anticipate any possible malfunction that might affect the operation the basic law of the industry is that:

'If something can go wrong, it will go wrong – and at the least convenient moment!'

It is for that reason that, so far, the view has been that the human brain is still the best computer for dealing with unforeseen problems – or indeed multiple problems such as those encountered by that Vanguard crew at Edinburgh.[2]

However, that is changing as the ever-increasing volume of traffic gives less opportunity for individual freedom. It is currently difficult to believe that passengers would be happy to board an aeroplane controlled remotely from the ground but accountants would be delighted if the cockpit crew was reduced to one superintendent of a remotely controlled system. The question then arises of how

2 See p.137

such a person would acquire the experience to recognise a deviation together with the skills necessary for corrective action.

The commercial airline pilot's life is not without its disadvantages. Passengers expect flights to be available to them round the clock every day of the year. Crew members cannot guarantee to be available for weekends, bank holidays or family and social events. Peak holiday seasons are the busiest time for airlines and therefore the least likely periods for crew to be allowed leave. Christmas and New Year may be spent thousands of miles from family. Pilots are not immune to jet lag and the most testing part of a flight is the arrival at destination after a long duty. (The most dangerous part is undoubtedly the drive home after being up all night!).

Pilots also have to accept that every movement of a modern commercial airliner is being recorded and sometimes even being transmitted back to home base. Every word spoken on the flight deck is recorded. If anything untoward happens on a flight these recordings will be pored over and spun by lawyers with little understanding of the industry but desperate to protect commercial interests. To that must be added the new threat of misadventures within minutes becoming viral fodder round the internet.

For all that, there are many compensations. The glory of soaring above the clouds after a gloomy winter departure. The majesty of mountain ranges on a sunny day. By night the magic of stars and aurora borealis above or the glittering lights of a city spread below. The satisfaction of bringing your passengers safely and professionally to their destination despite all the challenges weather and the system can throw at you. There are few professions where you can embark on a project and complete it in a single day.

My generation was passionate about flying and lucky to enjoy a golden era in aviation. Pilot status may have declined but there are still many thousands of young people who have the motivation to accept the disadvantages outlined above for the job satisfaction of doing something they love. For the budding pilot perhaps, that passion could be the most important quality of all.

Appendix 1

Early aviation in Scotland

Given the national traditions of engineering and innovation it is no surprise that aviation had come early to Scotland, one of several countries where early pioneers worked with gliders while waiting patiently for an engine powerful and light enough to give promise of sustained flight in a heavier-than-air machine.

Airship R34 above the huge shed which once stood at Inchinnan (close by the current Glasgow Airport).

Scottish aviation historians speculate wistfully about what might have been if naval architect Percy Pilcher's experiments had been not been cruelly cut short by the fatal crash of his Bat glider in 1899. He was only 32. Despite competing claims from other parts of the world, it was the Wright Brothers who took their place in the aviation hall of fame for the winning of that particular race in 1903.

It was the summer of 1910 before James Radley gave Scotland its first demonstration of powered flight in the grounds of Pollok House in Glasgow. A couple of months later he was one of twenty-two pilots who took part in Scotland's first flying meeting at Lanark Race Course. Over a week in August, over 200,000 people flocked to see such famous pioneers as the showman Samuel Franklin Cody. At Farnborough in October 1908 he had made a hop of 424 metres in his British Army Aeroplane No 1 which is accepted as being the first flight of a heavier-than-air machine in the British Isles.

In that year of 1908 the brothers Frank and Harold Barnwell of Balfron were among several Scots who had begun experimenting with aeroplanes. By 1911, their monoplane had flown five miles at 200 feet and Harold won a prize for a half mile flight in an all-Scottish aeroplane. Their efforts are commemorated by a cairn near the Wallace Monument in Stirling.

One of the few redeeming features of the senseless slaughter of WWI was that the endless extravagance involved did at least result in an explosion of aircraft development. Scotland's industry played its part, with companies like G & J Weir and William Beardmore adapting expertise in marine engineering to the production of aircraft under licence. In 1906, Beardmore had expanded from his company's industrial base at Parkhead Forge into shipbuilding. Having created the largest shipyard on the Clyde at Dalmuir, he diversified further into locomotives, heavy artillery and flying machines. The shipyard's contribution of over 70 ships to Britain's naval fleet ranged from submarines to dreadnoughts and included what is claimed to be the world's first aircraft carrier, HMS *Argus*. In addition to massive naval guns, the company produced over 500 howitzers and fifty tanks.

On the aviation side, the Royal Aircraft Factory's BE2c was built under licence. Although Beardmore produced their own design variations on that much maligned machine, they proved no more successful than the original. They had better luck with the Beardmore WBIII (their version of the Sopwith Pup), of which about a hundred were supplied to the Royal Naval Air Service. In total, the factory at Dalmuir produced over 800 aeroplanes but none seemed to have the promise of Beardmore's other great venture into aviation – the airship. These were built in a huge hangar at Inchinnan by the current Glasgow International Airport; their design much influenced by the study of captured German Zeppelins.

After the war, 1919 proved to be a landmark year in the history of British aviation. Cpt. John Alcock and his navigator Lt. Arthur Whitten Brown made the first non-stop West–East crossing of the Atlantic. In a converted Vickers Vimy bomber they left Lester Field near St Johns, Newfoundland, at 1.45 p.m. on 14 June 1919 and, after some hair-raising narrow escapes along the way, arrived at Clifden, Connemara some sixteen hours later. The landing was something of an anti-climax for the Vimy tipped on its nose when the green field which had looked such a promising site from the air turned out to be marshland. Nevertheless, Alcock and Brown won a prize of £10,000, became celebrated heroes and were knighted by King George V.[3]

Despite that achievement, many believed that prospects for future mass air travel would be better served by airships. This belief seemed to be reinforced when Beardmore's R34 made the first return crossing of the Atlantic in July of the same year. Setting off from her operational base at East Fortune on 2 July 1919 (barely a fortnight after the Vickers Vimy's epic flight), R34 arrived at Mineola, Long Island four and a half days later on the 6th.

Problems with wind, weather and engines had caused her captain, Major George Scott, to revise the Washington destination to Boston. However, after the British ground handling team made their way there it was decided that there was enough fuel remaining to reach New York. R34 made it with just an hour's endurance remaining but it meant there was now no one on the ground with experience of handling her. One of the crew members, Major J E M Pritchard, jumped by parachute to supervise the arrival thus becoming the first man ever to arrive in America after crossing the Atlantic by air.

The return flight departed on the 10th and with the assistance of the prevailing westerlies arrived in Pulham in Norfolk a mere 75 hours later on the 13th. However successful this might seem, the westbound time was little improvement on the record held by the infinitely more luxurious Cunard liner *Mauretania*. Eventually, the destruction of the underdeveloped and underpowered R101 at Beauvais in 1930 was to sound the death knell for British airships as passenger vehicles. Although Germany's Zeppelins were superior, the *Hindenburg* disaster of 1937 at Lakehurst, New Jersey effectively ended the passenger airship era.

For those who pinned their faith on heavier-than-air machines, 1919 saw the initial moves to set up aerial routes to the continent and beyond. Wartime bombers

---

3 As a sad footnote to the year, Sir John Alcock was killed on 18 December. He crashed in Normandy in atrocious weather conditions while attempting to complete a solo delivery of a new Vickers Viking amphibian for a Paris aeronautical exhibition. He was only 27.

were modified to carry passengers and negotiations began to secure international over-flying and landing rights. While Paris was an obvious first choice destination for an air service, the potential shortening of longer journey times was an enticing prospect for Britain's far-flung empire.

The early biplanes carried a handful of passengers in basic cabins which offered accommodation primitive by today's standards. Often the pilot would be in an open cockpit with all that entailed in terms of exposure to the elements. Initially, radio and navigation facilities were non-existent so the pioneers relied on features on the ground as they made their way. While that might be fairly straightforward in good weather, it could be infinitely more challenging in poor visibility and precipitation. Major roads and railway lines were particularly useful, with the latter offering the additional bonus of having station names visible to the low flying aviator. (This technique took its name from the Bradshaw railway timetables of the period, spawning the verb 'to Bradshaw'). All the time the prudent pilot kept a vigilant eye on adjacent open spaces which might prove useful in the event of a forced landing. An article in *Motor* magazine of 1910 speculated on what the transport scene might be like in 1960. While predicting fairly accurately the motorways of today, it assumed that wide grassy strips would be provided on either side as emergency landing fields for massive biplanes using them as primary navigation aids. To be fair, anyone suggesting in 1910 that in fifty years passengers would be crossing the Atlantic in jets travelling at over 500 miles per hour would have been dismissed as a romantic lunatic.

By August 1919, two companies were vying for the honour of operating the first passenger scheduled service between London and Paris. Officially, Aircraft Transport and Transport Limited were the winners on 25 August with a single-engined DH16 carrying four passengers. However, rivals Handley Page Transport Limited also flew to Le Bourget on the same day before inaugurating their own scheduled service a week later. Their contender was a converted HP 0/400 twin-engined bomber which could offer eight cane seats within the cabin together with the unbeatable attraction of a further two in the open cockpit next to the pilot!

1919 held at least one other significant event for Scotland. In May of that year, 25-year-old war hero William Sholto Douglas had gained the fourth British commercial licence ever issued. As part of his duties with Handley Page Transport Ltd, he flew over Dundee, Montrose and Aberdeen to drop bundles of newspapers by parachute. Thirty years later he was to become chairman of BEA.

Over the next five years, air services to the main cities of north west Europe were slowly built up until, in 1924, the early airlines were amalgamated with government help to form Imperial Airways. Predictably, the government input introduced bureaucracy and delay. The prime motivation for long haul services was the need for speedy communication with far flung empires. It was little surprise therefore that there was also keen interest in France, Belgium, Germany and Italy.

In Britain, the RAF had already set up air links to stations abroad. In the spring of 1925 the deHavilland test pilot, Alan Cobham, set off with Sir Sefton Brancker in a single-engined DH 50 biplane to survey possible landing sites for a commercial air service to India. Having successfully completed flights of 4,000 miles each way, he departed again in November of that year on a route-proving exercise to Capetown (twice as far). The return 8,000 mile journey took sixteen days (beating the liner SS *Windsor Castle* by two days) arriving back in Croydon on 13 March 1926. On 30 June he set off again for Australia – his DH50 now equipped with floats. As though the difficulties of pioneering navigation were not enough, his engineer was shot and killed as they overflew the desert between Baghdad and Basra. Undeterred, he borrowed an engineer from the RAF and flew on to Sydney and a rapturous reception from 60,000 people. Even greater crowds greeted his return to London at the end of July when, in dramatic fashion, he landed on the Thames by the Houses of Parliament. The next day he was knighted by King George V.

In the 30s, Cobham started to experiment with in-flight refuelling. Development was interrupted by the war but in the late 40s his company introduced the probe and drogue system of in-flight refuelling which has so extended the range of military aircraft.

Shortly before his death in 1973, I had the privilege of carrying him as a passenger. He was a very welcome guest on the flight deck.